[d i g i t a l]
CHARACTER
ANIMATION 3

New Riders

George Maestri

Digital Character Animation 3
George Maestri

New Riders
1249 Eighth Street
Berkeley, CA 94710
510/524-2178
800/283-9444
510/524-2221 (fax)

Find us on the Web at: www.newriders.com
To report errors, please send a note to errata@peachpit.com

New Riders is an imprint of Peachpit, a division of Pearson Education

Project Editors: Erin Kissane, Kristin Kalning
Development Editor: Erin Kissane
Production Editor: Lupe Edgar
Copy Editor: Rebecca Pepper
Tech Editor: Peter Richardson
Compositor: Kim Scott
Proofreader: Liz Welch
Indexer: Valerie Perry
Cover design: Aren Howell
Interior design: Maureen Forys

ISBN 0-321-37600-5

9 8 7 6 5 4 3 2 1

Printed and bound in the United States of America

Dedication

This book is dedicated to Victoria.

Acknowledgements

I'd like to thank Moyet and Preston for being such great kids and Alex for keeping my feet warm. I'd also like to acknowledge all the people at Peachpit who made this book happen: Kristin Kalning, Erin Kissane, Peter Richardson, Rebecca Pepper, Lupe Edgar, Maureen Forys, and Liz Welch. Thanks to Angie Jones for images used in Chapter 6. Special thanks to Lynda Weinman for being a great friend and for reconnecting me at Peachpit. Finally, I'd like to thank all the people over the years who helped teach me the art of animation.

Table of Contents

Chapter 10   Directing and Filmmaking   266

CHAPTER ONE

Basics of Character Design

This book is about creating characters and bringing them to life. Character creation includes a number of technical tasks, such as modeling, texturing, and rigging, all of which will be covered later. Before you start building a character, however, you'll need to design it.

Design is about making choices, both artistic and technical. It means getting to know your character's personality and then making choices that communicate this personality visually. When designing, you need to make decisions about size, shape, color, texture, clothing, and many other attributes. There is also a technical aspect to character design: well-designed characters are easy to animate, making the animator's job easier and more creative.

Good character design is one of the cornerstones of good animation. Designing your characters properly will make their personalities jump off the screen. Your audience will know who your characters are immediately—and like them. When you pair a great design with a great personality, the results can be wonderful.

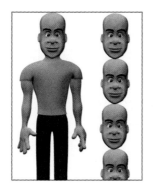

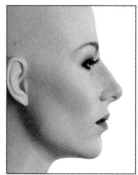

Approaching Design as an Artist

Character design is a very creative process and—as with any creative process—you can approach it from a number of directions. Your particular approach will depend a lot on your strengths as an artist. Some people like to sketch, some like to sculpt, and some prefer to design directly on the computer. Each method has its advantages, but you do need to keep in mind that your final product will be modeled in 3D.

However it's created, a well-designed character oozes personality. Your characters should be well proportioned and appealing to the eye. Even the villain should be appealing—particularly if it is in a delightfully gruesome way. If the audience doesn't identify with the character in some way, they'll lose interest.

Character design can be done for its own sake, or it can be done to meet a specific need. Many artists design characters simply to create interesting images, often without a story or a purpose for the character in mind. Because a great character can inspire all sorts of stories, design sometimes precedes all other elements of a project.

In other situations, you'll have a specific reason to design a character: to work within an existing story or sell a product, for example. In these cases, it's best to learn a bit about the character that you'll be designing before you start brainstorming.

When you're working within the constraints of an existing story, form should follow function. Understanding your character's function in the story will help you decide what form it needs to take. You might want to write down some of the distinguishing characteristics of your characters. What's the character's age? Personality? Size? How does your character relate to the other characters in the story? Is there an existing style? All of these factors play a role in the character's final design.

A character designed to sell a product may use the product itself as the starting point, such as this package of chewing gum.

The Creative Process

The design process always starts with creative inspiration, which is then refined and developed into a full character design. This design is typically a drawing or sculpture that describes the character in detail so it can be modeled digitally in 3D.

An explanation of the creative process could easily fill a separate book, but there are a few simple things you can do to tap into the creative side of your brain. Creativity is a flow of ideas that your brain connects in unexpected ways to form new ideas, and keeping these ideas flowing can be tricky. Any critique shuts down the creative flow, so try to avoid criticizing your work during the creative process. Critique is important, but should happen during revision, not creation.

Working in a medium you're comfortable with also helps. Sketching works well for me because it feels natural and I don't have to think about it. When I'm on the computer, things can get technical very quickly, which breaks the creative flow. Besides, pencils are fast and paper is cheap. It's much faster and more economical to generate ideas on paper than using a technical 3D application.

Idle sketches can inspire new character designs. Always be on the lookout for new ideas for characters.

Technical Considerations

As you design, you do need to keep technical considerations in mind. Someone designing for a game, for instance, will need to limit designs to a specific number of polygons so the game engine doesn't choke. This technical limitation fundamentally affects the design and forces it to stay simple. Adding details like realistic hair and clothing will create additional work, increasing the production budget and extending the schedule.

Use the strong points of your software to your advantage, and design around its limitations. Make sure your character is easy to deform and animate; a character that's hard to animate can blow a budget very quickly.

A solid understanding of the technical issues involved in 3D animation is gained through experience. When you're starting out, you'll probably need to ask a lot of questions of more experienced animators. For your own initial projects, it's best to keep your designs simple so you don't get bogged down in technical problems.

The simple hair on this character took a few minutes to render. These minutes can add up significantly when rendering a long scene. Changing the hair to a stylized design cut the render time down to a few seconds.

Realistic clothing can be another big technical challenge.

Using Reference

Good reference is always handy during the design process. Get outside into nature or look at other design, art, and film for inspiration. If you're designing a creature, you may want to take a trip to the zoo to find animals to use as reference. The Internet is also a terrific resource. A Google image search, for example, can produce all sorts of great reference images to use as inspiration.

Refining Your Design

Once you hit upon a good idea, you'll need to refine it into conceptual art, which then needs to be refined further into a final character design. You may need to redraw or resculpt the character many times before it works for the production. This is also the point where you need to ask whether the design is feasible in terms of budget and technical requirements.

Designing a giraffe? A trip to the zoo with your camera or some Internet research can get you plenty of inspiration.

Design Styles

Design falls into two very broad categories—realistic and stylized—with a lot of gray area in between. Realistic designs mimic nature as closely as possible, while stylized designs caricature reality. Your decisions about how realistic you want your characters to be will affect every part of the filmmaking process.

Realistic Characters

If you want to create characters that closely mimic reality, then digital animation is certainly the medium you should choose. Feature-film animators and special effects teams can create characters and creatures that look completely real and integrate them into live-action environments.

Realism, however, comes with a price tag. The rule of thumb is that the more realistic something is, the more difficult it will be to animate. This is particularly true for realistic humans. Audience members interact with people every day and are experts in human behavior, so they will pick up on anything even slightly "off" about a realistic human character. While you might be able to get away with realistic humans in crowd scenes and as virtual stuntmen without a lot of extra effort, the more screen time the characters get, the more work you'll have to do to sell a realistic character to the audience.

Getting a still 3D model to look real is a much different task than getting the same model to move convincingly.

When considering realism, make sure you don't bite off more than you can chew. Nothing looks creepier to an audience than a realistic character that doesn't move realistically; that last 10 percent of realism takes more than 90 percent of the effort.

Stylized Characters

Stylizing a character avoids some of the problems involved with realism. If a character doesn't look completely photorealistic, the audience will be more willing to accept unrealistic movement and expression. This gives you the opportunity to write your own rules for the character and the world.

This stylized dog doesn't really look like a canine, but the audience will accept it.

A good example of stylized designs can be drawn from the classic cartoons of the 1940s. Daffy Duck hardly looks like a real duck, but he's certainly a very real character. Daffy moves in a very stylized way, and his body can stretch to cartoon extremes, but the audience accepts these wild motions because that's how Daffy's world works.

3D animation can certainly mimic reality, but animation is always at its best when it creates its own reality. A caricatured design, however, is not a license to animate your characters poorly. Good animation will make even the simplest character seem to live and breathe.

Stylized doesn't have to mean cartoony. A creature for a science fiction movie may look photorealistic, but is stylized in its own way. Even if the designer is inspired by nature, the end result is a new, stylized version of reality. This is the gray area between stylization and reality. Since the audience has never seenz this creature, you can decide how it will behave—but if the character looks realistic, its behavior should feel correspondingly realistic to the audience.

Cartoony characters can squash and stretch to extremes without losing audience acceptance.

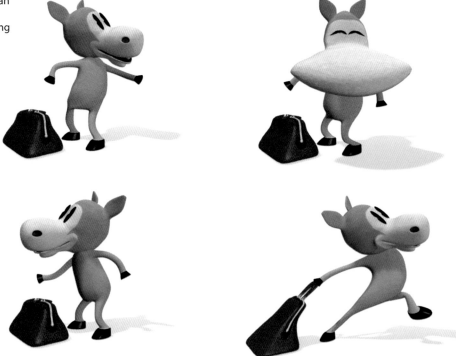

Designing a Character

A character's design will depend largely on the character's personality and its role in the film. A character that is big and mean might have broad shoulders and beady eyes; a character with big eyes and a potbelly will seem meek in comparison. The relative proportions of your characters can tell the audience a lot about them.

Head and Body Proportions

Perhaps the most important proportion in a character design is the ratio of the head to the body. An average adult human is seven to eight heads tall, while an infant may be only a few heads tall. If the character is taller than average, it may look more lithe, graceful, or powerful, like a fashion model or superhero.

Stylized characters can have larger heads in relation to their bodies. One reason their heads are often larger is that the head and face communicate a lot of information about the character's mood and personality, and a bigger head makes these features more readable to the audience.

A **realistic human** stands about 7 to 8 heads tall. Exaggerated characters, such as body-builders, superheroes, and fashion models, may be as many as 9 or 10 heads tall. A **stylized human** usually has a slightly exaggerated head, making the character 4 to 5 heads tall. This makes the face bigger and more readable. A **highly stylized character** may have a head that's almost as big as its body.

Faces

The face is the very center of your character, and a good design will instantly tell the audience who the character is and what the character is feeling. Faces can take on a huge variety of shapes, and achieving this flexibility is a formidable design task as well as a technical and modeling challenge.

Make sure your character has enough room for the features to move around within the face. Some characters have an expression fixed on their faces; if your character is perpetually sunny or grumpy, don't hesitate to put this into the design.

Eyes

The eyes are the windows to the soul, and your character's eyes will give the audience a lot of information. Because eyes are so important, many designers make them quite large so the audience can see them more clearly. This is particularly true in genres like anime, in which the eyes can take up almost half the head. The size of the eyes in relation to the face also gives clues to the character's personality. Typically, larger eyes are cuter and more child-like, whereas small, beady eyes may indicate a villain.

Eyes express emotion mainly through the lids, which can narrow or widen to change the shape of the eyes. Many characters have eyes modeled as part of the face, but some use "clamshell" lids: essentially half-spheres used much like a puppet's eyes. Other characters simply use replacement animation, in which different expressions are swapped in as needed, to create the eyes.

The eyes of your character can also change shape. If your character has cartoon eyes, you can bend and flex the eyes dramatically to indicate the character's emotions. If your character has eyes that sit inside the head and behave more realistically, you won't have as much freedom in changing the shape when it's animation time.

Animal eyes can be tricky to design because many animals have eyes on the side of their head. This can make the animation task of conveying emotion difficult because the audience can see only one eye at a time. Many designers stylize animal eyes by "humanizing" them and moving them toward the front of the face.

The eyes on the left use clamshell lids, which are easy to construct and animate but not as realistic as the lids on the right, which are part of the face.

This simple set of eyes can squash and stretch for more cartoony effects.

In the real world, many animals have eyes on the side of their head, such as the fish on the left. To design eyes that are more expressive, move them toward the front to "humanize" them.

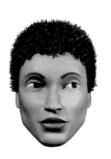

Realistic eyebrows are modeled as part of the surface of the face.

Brows

A character's brows work in concert with the eyes to convey emotion. Raising the brows might indicate surprise, while lowering them might indicate anger. Creating good brow motion is very important, and your design will affect the way your brows work.

Realistic character designs model the brow as part of the surface of the face. To manipulate the brows, a modeler may need to create a number of different shapes or "morph targets" that can be blended or morphed together to create animation. Other characters use design to work around this complexity, creating cartoon brows that float on the surface of the face—or, in extreme cases, float above it.

Mouths

The mouth can be highly expressive and take on a huge variety of shapes, so proper design is very important. Most characters have mouths that are integral to the surface of the face. As with eyes and brows, this makes the creation of proper shapes and morph targets a significant modeling task. Some characters sidestep this issue and use replacement animation for the mouths, which isn't realistic but can lend the project a stop-motion feel.

Stylized brows can be modeled as separate geometry that floats on the surface of the face.

Extremely stylized brows don't even have to be attached to the face.

Mouths can take a wide variety of shapes. Be sure to plan for this when designing.

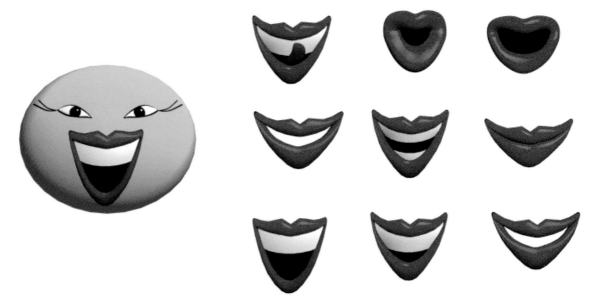

Some animators use replacement mouths that simply replace the character's entire mouth, a technique used frequently in stop-motion, cut-out, and clay animation.

Here we have a character whose hand and body are one seamless mesh.

Hands

Outside of the face, the hands are probably the most expressive part of the body. Many characters gesture a lot with their hands, and a well-designed hand will allow your character to express itself more clearly. As with heads, you can use slightly oversized hands on a stylized character for a cartoony look. If your design is more realistic, you'll want to proportion the hands realistically as well.

One challenge with hands is attaching the hand to the arm or the wrist. This is an extremely flexible joint, and proper deformations can be tricky. A long sleeve or wristband can be used to hide a seam, which allows you to create the hand separately and avoid this technical problem.

This character hides the seam under the sleeve, which may simplify deformation and rigging of the character.

If you want, you can give your character cartoon gloves for hands. In the 1920s and '30s, animators found that white gloves made their characters' hands easier to see and therefore more expressive. For a 3D animator, cartoon gloves can serve the same purpose, while also hiding a telltale seam.

Segmenting Characters

Many characters are built using a single mesh. Although this is a natural way to create a character, it forces you to deform every part of the mesh when you animate the character. Mesh deformation is always a little problematic and can be resource-intensive, so sometimes breaking your character into manageable parts can simplify the rigging and animation process. It's very easy to design collars, clothing, and other accessories to help hide seams for your characters.

Some characters are designed from the ground up as segmented characters. A character such as a robot would actually be built with body parts as individual objects and might not even need mesh deformation at the joints. This makes the setup and rigging of the character very straightforward.

A cartoon glove is stylish, and it helps you design around the tricky problem of seamlessly attaching your character's hand to the wrist.

A segmented character like this robot is built out of individual parts, eliminating the need for mesh deformation.

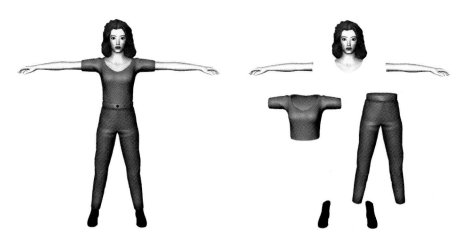

Even organic meshes can be segmented. A neck can be hidden under a collar, while clothing can hide other joints.

Finalizing Your Design

The ultimate goal of the design process is to create an image or sculpture that can be used as a reference to model the character in a 3D application. 3D modeling can be a very technical pursuit, so the art you create must be technically precise. Think of technical drawings used in industry and architecture; this is essentially what you will be creating. To model a character, you will need at least two orthographic views: side and front. These can be created using drawings, sculptures, or photographs.

Drawing Your Characters

People who draw often "cheat" the third dimension. This little guy looks fine on a flat sheet of paper, but he might not transfer well to 3D.

The simplest way to finalize your character designs is to sketch them on paper. A pencil is a wonderful thing, because it allows you to very quickly block out the size and shape of your character. If you know how to write your name, you can most likely draw a character.

If you spend much time modeling characters on the computer, you'll develop a visual sense that will translate to paper as well. The act of modeling characters seems to improve your drawing, while drawing characters improves your modeling. Another way to improve both skills is through a life drawing class, which is the single best way to understand the aesthetics of the human form.

The Problem with 2D

The one problem with drawings is that they are 2D representations of a 3D world. Many artists "cheat" the third dimension when drawing, and while this works within the drawing, translating that to 3D can be difficult. When creating drawings for modeling, you need to make sure they don't cheat and are accurate to 3D.

Finalizing Your Drawings

The final drawings that prepare your character for modeling need to be very accurate technical drawings that work in 3D. Creating accurate front and side views of a character is not as easy as it sounds. Each view must line up precisely with the other drawings once they're scanned into the computer.

The drawings also need to have very specific poses. At a minimum, you'll want a front and side view, but top and back views can also be helpful for some characters. Draw your characters with the arms outstretched in the front view, to assist in modeling and rigging the arms. If your character is symmetrical, be sure to make the drawing symmetrical. One way to ensure that your character is symmetrical is to draw only half the character on paper, scan it, and then flip it in Photoshop to create the other half.

These are nice drawings, but they do very little to help the modeler realize the character.

This is much better. The character has front and side views, the arms are extended, and the front view is symmetrical.

These images can be mapped onto planes in a 3D application and used as a reference for modeling the character.

Sculpting Your Characters

Another way to design characters is to sculpt them in clay. A 3D clay sculpture is much closer to the final character than any 2D drawing can get. Clay, however, is messier, more difficult to model accurately, and certainly a great deal more time-consuming than sketching.

Like drawing, sculpting is an art. Plenty of books and classes are available to teach the finer points of sculpture. If you understand 3D modeling, you should take to sculpture quite easily, and you'll probably find the interactivity of clay far superior to that of any computer-driven interface.

Once you've created an acceptable sculpture, there are two methods for getting it into the computer for modeling. The first method is simply to take a photograph of the sculpture. The second is to digitize the actual surface of the model, using a 3D scanner or digitizer. The method you choose will depend on your needs and also your budget. Laser scanning is very accurate and makes modeling easier, but the process can get expensive because it's usually done by an outside service. Digital cameras make photographing a subject very easy, and good reference photos are typically enough to create an accurate model.

The camera needs to be placed so it is shooting perpendicular to the subject.

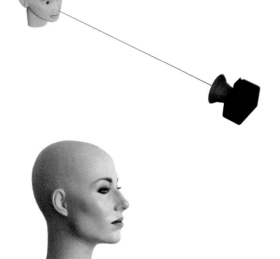

This shot is not perpendicular, and the result is a less than perfect profile.

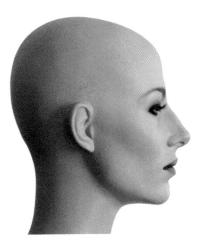

This shot is dead-on and will make modeling the profile much easier.

Photographing Sculpture

You can photograph a sculpture for reference, but you can also photograph just about anything else: if you want to model a likeness of real person or an animal, for example, you can photograph them instead of sculpting or drawing them. Regardless of the subject, the process is pretty much the same. Like making a technical drawing, taking an accurate photograph that can be used for 3D modeling requires a bit of care.

When photographing a 3D object for modeling, you will always need to get accurate front and side views. The photographs you create will need to mimic the front and side orthographic views in your 3D program. To accomplish this, position the camera so that it is level with and pointing straight at the object being photographed. If the camera is too high or low or off to one side, the object will be distorted, making it difficult to model. When photographing a head, for example, it's usually best to center the camera on the subject's nose. You also need to maintain a uniform distance between the lens and the subject for each view. The best way to do this is to put the camera on a tripod and back the subject up against a wall to create a fixed distance between the two.

Another important parameter is the focal length of the lens. A long lens flattens your subject, mimicking an orthographic view and providing a more accurate modeling reference. To better understand this, think of a fisheye lens, which is the opposite of a long lens. A fisheye intentionally distorts the subject, making modeling harder. If your camera has a variable zoom, zoom all the way in and move the camera back to frame your subject.

This front view was shot with a wide 28mm lens, which distorts the perspective, causing a slight fisheye effect.

Moving the camera back and zooming the lens to 100mm flattens the perspective, making the image more accurate and more like the orthographic viewpoints used in modeling.

Preparing Photographs for Modeling

Preparing a set of photographs for modeling follows much the same process as getting a set of drawings ready. The photographs are transferred or scanned into a computer. Even the most careful photo session will create images that are slightly different in size, so an image-editing application such as Photoshop is useful for scaling and arranging the photos.

These photos were aligned in Photoshop. A few guidelines can help align the images.

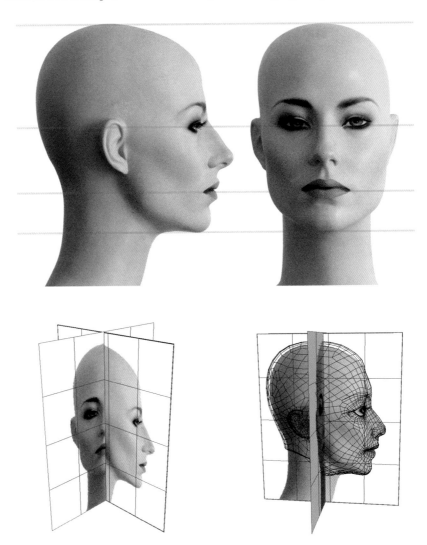

Once the images are aligned, they can be **mapped** to reference planes. With the planes as a reference, the **modeling** will be accurate to the design.

Character Design

In this first exercise, you get to design a simple character. Take a pencil and paper, and sketch out some character designs that you might want to model in the next few chapters. (If you're more familiar with sculpting, you might want to do this in clay.) These designs should focus on the outward appearance of the character and its proportions, and whether the character is small, large, skinny, fat, and so on.

Once you have a number of designs, look carefully at each character and think of how it might be constructed in your chosen software. Since you are just getting started, these issues may not be readily apparent. Your design may change as you learn more about how to build characters. Find a design that you like, and create a set of technical drawings or photographs to get your character ready for the modeling process, which will be covered in the next chapter.

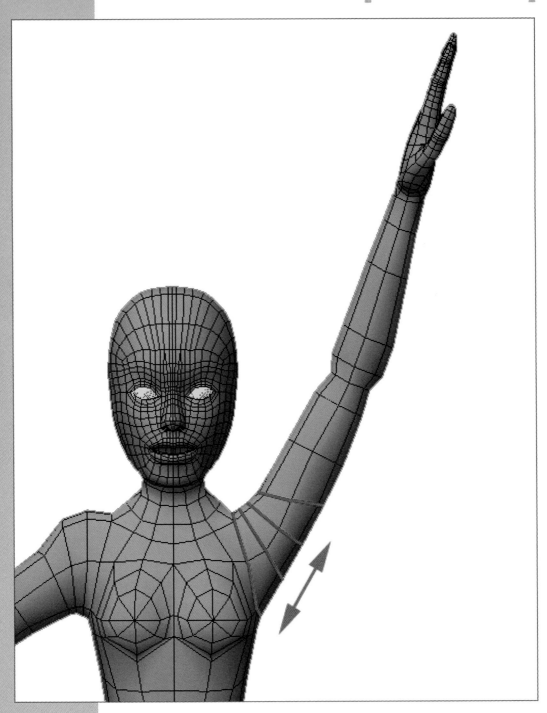

CHAPTER TWO

Modeling Characters

After you've designed your character, you need to turn it into a 3D model.
This model will certainly need to look good, but it must also meet some technical requirements. Most models need to be deformed during animation, so
your model must be constructed in a way that allows it to deform naturally
and easily. Building your character properly before you start animating will
save you headaches in the long run.

Modeling is an art unto itself, and in many ways, it's like digital sculpting.
Becoming a good sculptor requires a good eye—and a good grasp of volume and form. And, as with all arts that center on the human form, it's a
big help if you have a good understanding of anatomy. Taking time to learn
sculpting in a physical medium, such as clay, can also improve your digital
sculpting skills.

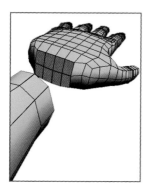
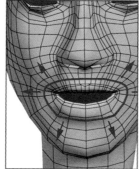

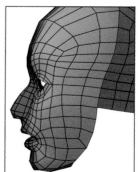

Surface Types

When modeling, you can use many different surfaces to create a character, including polygons, subdivision surfaces, and NURBS-based surfaces. (I'll explain what these are later.) The type of surface you choose depends on a number of factors. One of these factors is the software package you're using. If your software supports only polygonal surfaces, your decision is already made—the character must be built out of polygons. Some packages are more adept at one type of modeling than others: a package with more tools for manipulating NURBS surfaces might make NURBS the best choice for your character. The type of project may also play a role in your choice of surfaces. A character in a gaming environment, for example, may need to be built from polygons simply because most game engines support polygons.

Polygonal Surfaces

Polygonal modeling was the first form of 3D modeling developed for computer graphics. Although more sophisticated modeling techniques have since been developed, basic polygonal modeling remains the most effective technique to use in many situations. Polygonal models are simple to construct, and they can be used in almost any situation, from feature films to games. Polygons are simply triangles or rectangles, each representing a plane and defining an area of the character's surface. All other forms of modeling resolve to polygons at some point, usually before rendering.

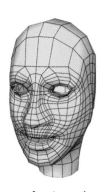

A human face is another fairly complex surface because it has holes for the eyes, mouth, and nostrils. Again, polygons handle these complex surfaces easily.

One big benefit of polygonal modeling is the freedom you have when constructing a character. Patch modeling, the other popular form of modeling, can limit you to surfaces that are topologically simple, such as a plane, cylinder, or sphere. In order to create an object that's more complex, such as a body, you'll need to attach multiple surfaces together. Polygons don't suffer from this topological constraint, and with a polygonal modeler, you're free to make your surface as complex as you desire. Another advantage of polygonal modeling is simplicity: a polygonal model often consists of a single object, but NURBS models, the most common form of patch models, are frequently composed of dozens of patch objects, therefore adding complexity to the whole project.

The downfall of polygonal modeling is that a polygon is by definition a plane, so you'll need many small polygons to create a smoothly curved surface.

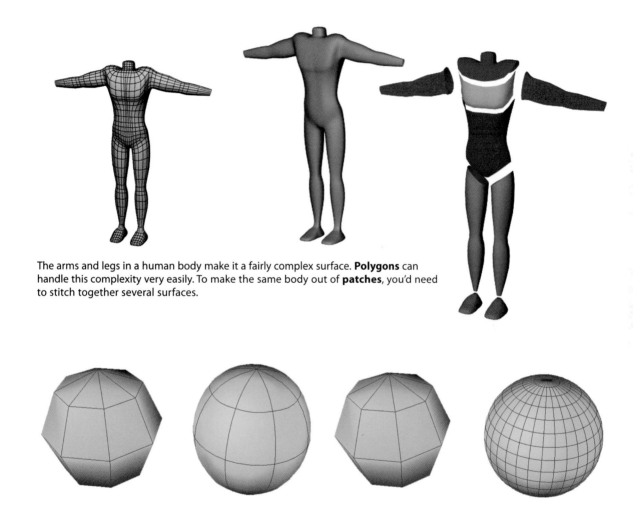

The arms and legs in a human body make it a fairly complex surface. **Polygons** can handle this complexity very easily. To make the same body out of **patches**, you'd need to stitch together several surfaces.

The polygonal sphere on the left is not nearly as smooth as the NURBS sphere on the right.

For the polygonal sphere to be smooth, it needs a lot more detail, in the form of more polygons. This added detail slows down the animation process, however.

Working with Polygons

Since polygons are the fundamental building blocks of all 3D animation, most 3D modeling packages use some form of polygonal modeling. The underlying concepts of polygonal modeling are the same in all packages, though they do differ in interface and workflow.

Elements of a Polygonal Model

Polygonal models are built of vertices (points) that define edges (lines), which in turn define polygons or faces (planes). You can create and manipulate these geometric building blocks using a variety of relatively standardized tools.

Basic Polygonal Operations

An extrusion takes a vertex, edge, or polygon and extrudes the component, adding additional detail and pushing or pulling it into or away from the surface. A bevel adds one or more polygons that are at an angle to the original geometry. Most packages allow you to define the angle of the bevel and the height of the new detail above or below the original surface. A collapse reduces a face or edge to a single vertex. A cut slices a face into two parts, adding an edge and splitting the polygon in two. The cut may or may not be symmetrical.

A **vertex** is a single point. An **edge** is a two-dimensional line connecting two vertices. A **polygon**, or face, is a three-dimensional plane defined by three or more edges or vertices.

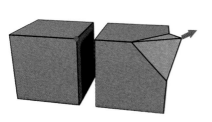

An **extruded vertex**

An **extruded edge**

An **extruded face**

A **beveled vertex**

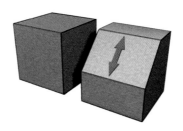

A **beveled edge**

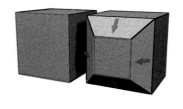

A **beveled face**

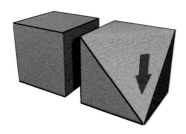

A **collapsed edge**

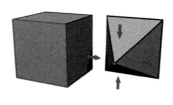

A **collapsed face**

A **cut face**

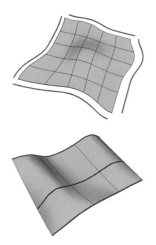

Patches and NURBS Surfaces

Patch surfaces are more complex than polygonal surfaces; while a polygon has straight lines for edges, a patch has curves for edges. These curves, in turn, define a curved surface. Since these surfaces are defined mathematically, they're also perfectly smooth. Think of a patch as a flexible sheet of rubber that can be bent and twisted into any shape. This makes patches a great choice for applications like car bodies or a character's skin, for which you need very smooth surfaces. Patch models can be created using individual patches or collections of patches that are stitched together into a seamless whole. Patches come in a number of different varieties, including Bézier patches and B-splines, but NURBS surfaces are by far the most common type of patches.

A patch surface is four-sided and defined by curves. Think of it as a rectangular sheet of rubber.

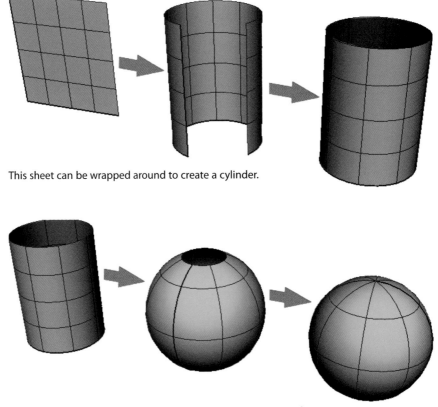

This sheet can be wrapped around to create a cylinder.

The ends of the cylinder can be brought together to create a sphere.

NURBS stands for non-uniform rational B-splines. NURBS patches allow for curved surfaces and also support such advanced features as vertex weighting, which allows you to define the curvature very precisely. These are by far the most popular types of patches and are supported by packages like Maya and Softimage.

The big limitation of patch-based modeling is that patches are always four-sided objects. Thus, to create a complex shape like a face or a body, you need to stitch several patches together. While many packages offer tools to automate this process, a stitched-together model can still be difficult to manage.

A more complex NURBS head must be created as a collection of individual patches, which are stitched together.

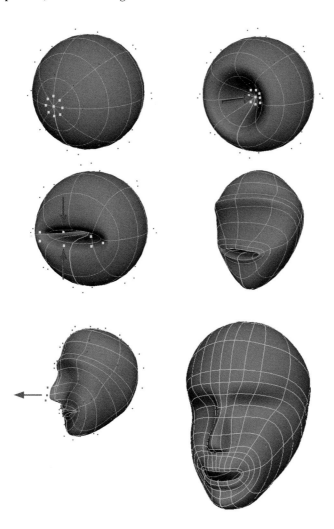

This head was created by deforming a simple NURBS sphere.

Working with Patches

Not all 3D modeling packages support patches, but those that do offer similar sets of tools to create and manipulate patch-based models. The type of patch used varies from package to package, and although NURBS has become the most popular patch type, some packages define their own types of patches. The best type of modeling to learn is probably NURBS modeling, but other surface types have their own advantages. Once you learn one type of patch modeling, learning the others will come more naturally.

Patch and Curve Types

Curves can come in many different forms, but they are all created from control points, which define the basic shape of the curve. The type of curve determines how these points are used. In modeling, you'll use curves to define patch surfaces, and the type of curves you use will determine what kind of patches you end up with.

Basic Patch Operations

You can create patches using a number of methods, all of which use the shape of one or more curves to define a more complex 3D surface. Some of these operations are used in very similar ways, but their subtle differences allow for more flexibility when modeling.

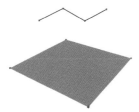

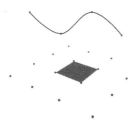

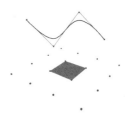

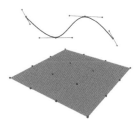

Linear—A first-degree curve, this looks like a series of lines connecting the control points. The resulting patch also has straight edges and is very similar to a polygonal surface.

Cardinal—A second-degree curve, this curve passes through the control points. The resulting patch will actually have control points beyond the edge of the surface.

B-spline—A third-degree curve, this type of curve rarely passes through its control points. The resulting patch also has control points beyond the edges.

Bézier—This curve passes through the control points, and each point has two tangents that are used to adjust the weight on either side of the point. A patch made out of Bézier curves will have a curved surface and also extend to the outer control points.

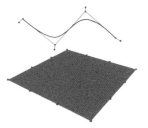

NURBS—This curve is like the B-spline, but with weighting that can pull the curve closer to the control point. The patch is very similar to a Bézier patch, but also has weighted control points.

Extrude—Sweeps a profile curve along a line or a path to create a surface.

Revolve/Lathe—Takes an outline curve and sweeps it around an axis to create a surface.

Skin—takes a series of sequential profile curves and uses them to progressively define the surface.

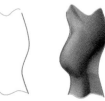

Loft—Uses a path curve and multiple profile curves to create a more complex surface than is possible with extruding or skinning.

Rule—Uses two curves to define opposite edges of the surface. This is often used to bridge the edges of adjacent surfaces.

BiRail—Constructs a surface by sweeping profile curves along two rail curves.

Boundary—Uses three or four curves to define the edges of a patch.

Subdivision Surfaces

Subdivision surfaces offer the best of both worlds. You can model them with polygonal modeling tools, so they can have any topology, but they resolve to very smooth surfaces at render time, just as patches do. Because of this ability, subdivision surfaces are fast becoming the standard method for modeling characters. All of the characters modeled in this book are modeled using polygonal tools so they can be animated quickly, but can also take advantage of subdivision surfaces for smooth final renders.

Subdivision surfaces are polygonal objects which can be dynamically and nondestructively smoothed into a high-resolution object for rendering. In most packages, this subdivision happens after the object is animated and before rendering. This means that your character rig will deform the low-res model, making animation fast and easy, while the renderer will see the high-res subdivided version of the same model.

Subdividing a surface progressively smooths it by adding detail.

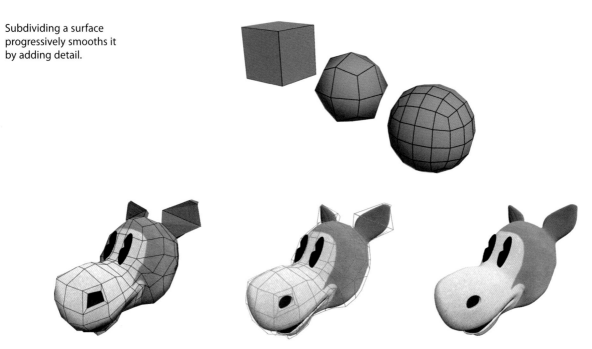

A **low-resolution** polygonal model of a head. When the model is turned into a **subdivision surface**, many software packages will display a "cage" that surrounds the surface and shows the original low-resolution model. This can make modeling much easier. When the model is **rendered**, the result is a smooth, subdivided surface without the cage.

When you subdivide a polygonal surface, the software needs to figure out where to place all of the added detail. These extra polygons are placed according to any number of formulas, but the simplest way of calculating this extra detail is by cutting some corners—literally. A woodcarver sculpting a block of wood would start by whittling off the corners of the block. If you mathematically whittle the corners off of your virtual character, you will also get a smoother surface. This technique is called "corner clipping."

Corner clipping connects the midpoints of your object's polygons with intermediate polygons—turning one polygon into four, four into sixteen, and so on. With each iteration, the corners are whittled away and the object gets smoother.

If you repeat the clipping process an infinite number of times, the resulting surface is exactly the same as a B-spline patch. Many implementations of subdivision surfaces also allow you to weight vertices to get corners that are sharper or more rounded. This weighting is very similar to NURBS. As you've seen, subdivision surfaces really do offer the best features of both worlds.

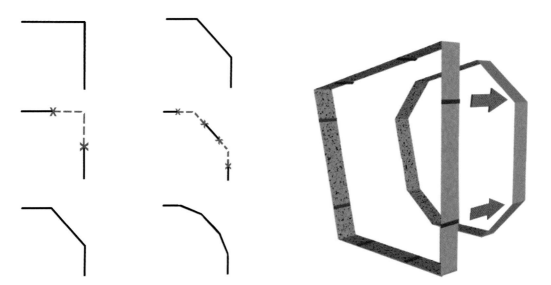

Take two simple lines, find the midpoints, and then cut the corners. **Repeat** as needed until the line approaches a curve.

In 3D, the theory is the same, but the faces are subdivided.

Creating Characters

Once you understand the basic geometry types and modeling tools, you can start modeling your character. We'll be building human-like characters constructed out of polygons that can be easily turned into subdivision surfaces.

Anatomy

As you build your character, you'll need to consider the underlying structure or anatomy of your character. Getting the surface to match the design is certainly important, but you'll also need to understand the character's muscles and skeleton because they affect the way the surface moves and deforms.

A good book on anatomy is always a great reference for modelers and animators alike. Another good way to get a strong foundation in anatomy is through life drawing classes. Learning to see the underlying structure helps train the eye and enhances your understanding of the human form. Those working with animals or creatures can also find plenty of references on animal anatomy.

Flexibility

A basic knowledge of anatomy will also help you ensure that your character is flexible. Knowing where joints will bend and how they bend can help you plan your model. Jointed areas typically need more detail to maintain a smooth outline as the joint bends. This detail, however, needs to be placed properly.

Another way to ensure flexibility is to keep your models light, which means to make your models as simple as possible and avoid unnecessary detail. A simpler surface is easier to deform and animates faster. The last thing you want is a noticeable wait while the screen updates each time you pose the character—real-time feedback is very important when animating. Ideally, you want to be able to pose the character as fast as you can think.

Knees and Elbows

Elbows, knees, and knuckles all move along a single axis, which makes them very simple to construct. When you model such a joint, it's a good idea to plan for this single-axis type of skin movement. The skin on the outside of the joint will expand, while the skin on the inside will compress. Model the detail in a slight fan shape to help with the expected deformation.

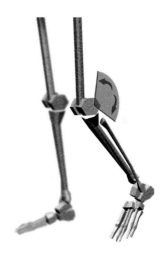

Elbows move along a single axis. **Knees** also are hinged joints.

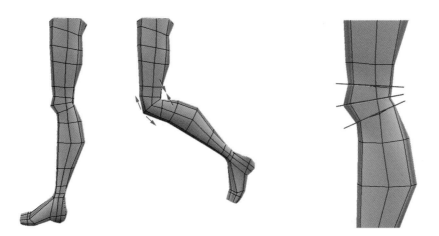

When a joint bends, the skin on the outside of the joint expands, while the skin inside compresses. To help with the deformation, it's sometimes helpful to **model the detail** surrounding the joint in a slight fan shape.

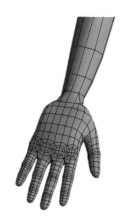

Wrists

Wrists are a little more complex. The wrist itself moves along two axes. The forearm consists of two bones, the radius and ulna. These bones twist around each other to allow the hand to turn along the third axis.

Hips

The hips allow the legs to move along two axes, rotating the thigh forward and to the side of the body. The most extreme motion occurs when the leg rotates forward, compressing and creasing the skin along the very top of the thigh.

Since the wrist can move in any direction, it's best to keep the detail fairly neutral. Make sure the forearm has enough detail to twist properly as well.

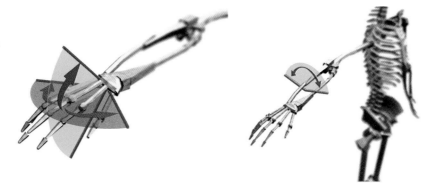

The **wrist** moves along two axes. The bones that make up the **forearm** twist to rotate the hand along the axis of the forearm.

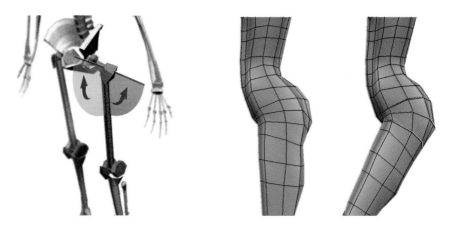

The **hips** move along two axes. **Bending the thigh forward** is the broadest motion of the hips. Aligning the detail in a fan shape can help this deformation.

Shoulders

Shoulders are by far the most complex area of the body to model, simply because the arms have such a wide range of motion. The upper arm moves along three axes, which makes proper deformation problematic for any model.

It's wise to consider the character's expected range of motion when you're modeling. If your character will keep his arms at his side most of the time, adjust the detail so the areas under the arm collapse properly. Conversely, if you have a superhero who is flying through the air with his arms out-stretched, you'll need to consider that as you model. Sometimes it's not possible to get a model that performs well under all circumstances, so you may need multiple models.

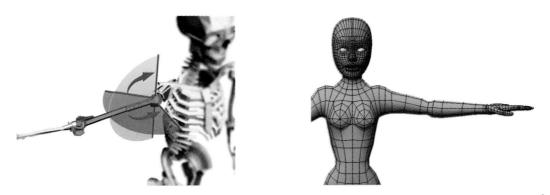

The **shoulders** have a very wide range of motion. Most models are created with the **arms outstretched**.

When the arms move down toward the charac-ter's side, we should get the familiar fan shape. As the character's **arms move up**, the fan shape reverses and we have a totally different shape. Getting this wide range of motion can be very tricky because of the chang-ing shapes.

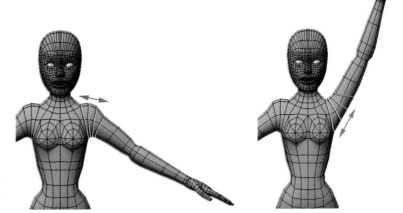

Spine

The spine can bend along all three axes, but most of the time the spine is used to bend characters at the waist. When modeling the torso, be sure to add enough detail so that the character bends smoothly, but not so much that the detail runs into itself and starts creasing.

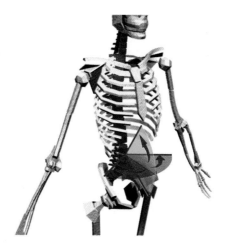

The spine allows the torso to bend and twist along all axes.

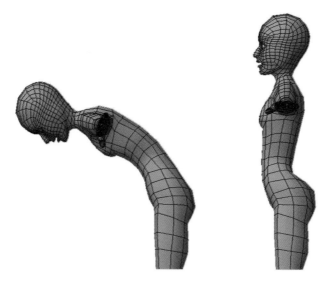

When modeling the torso, add enough detail so that it bends smoothly, but not so much that the detail starts creasing.

Modeling a Simple Body

Now that you understand the basics of modeling and how to place detail around the joints, it's time to start modeling.

The body we will model in this exercise is very simple, but it will be fairly flexible, anatomically correct, and easy to model. It uses a technique called box modeling, which starts with a simple box that you can refine into a basic model. This body is great for a stylized character.

Start with a **simple box** that has three vertical divisions and four horizontal ones. **Reshape the box** a little bit so that the middle column is narrower than the ends. **Select the polygons** on the bottom and extrude them to make leg stubs.

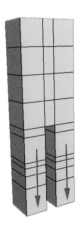  

Continue the extrusion to get the desired detail for the legs. **Reshape the legs** a bit. We will be subdividing the model a little later, so just get the general shape. **Select the polygons** along the top corners and extrude them to create arms.

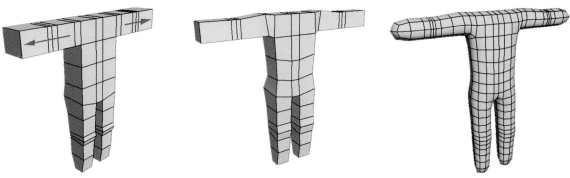

As with the legs, **keep extruding** to finish the arms. **Reshape** the arms and shoulders a bit. Now **subdivide or smooth** the model once. This will add more detail that can be used to refine the model.

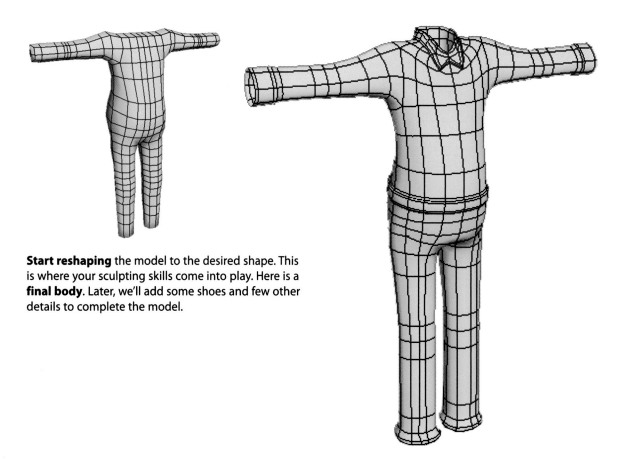

Start reshaping the model to the desired shape. This is where your sculpting skills come into play. Here is a **final body**. Later, we'll add some shoes and few other details to complete the model.

Modeling a Realistic Human Body

The body modeled here will be fairly realistic. As with life drawing, understanding how to create a realistic body will give you a good foundation for other, more stylized characters.

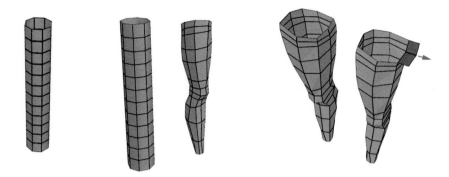

Start with an open-ended cylinder. Give yourself enough detail to model the leg. In this case, we used 12 subdivisions along the length and 8 radial subdivisions. **Resculpt the cylinder** to create a leg. Be sure to include enough detail around the knee to allow it to deform properly. **Select these two edges** along the top of the leg and extrude them slightly.

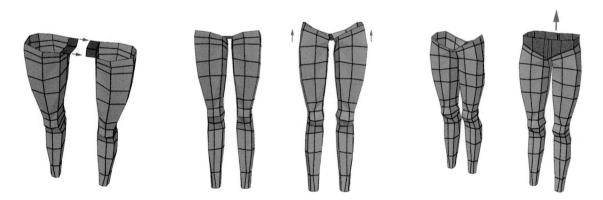

Duplicate the leg and mirror it. Attach or weld the extruded edges of the legs. **This creates the base** of our character's body. Before we create the body, reshape the tops of the legs to give a more natural outline. **The body is created** by selecting the edges surrounding the base of the torso and extruding them upward.

Keep extruding and reshaping as you go. **Continue** until you get to the base of the neck. Try to add only enough detail to define the shape of the character. If you have a reference drawing or photograph, you should compare your model to it frequently to maintain accuracy.

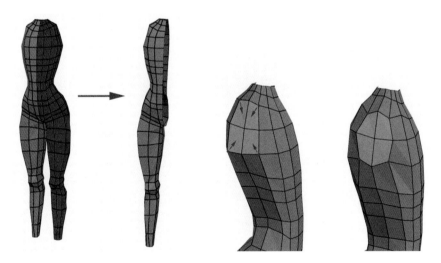

Since the character is symmetrical, we will **delete the left half** of the body to make modeling go faster. We can duplicate the right half later to create the left half. **Select these vertices** surrounding the arm socket. Round off the corners of these polygons to create the base of the arm.

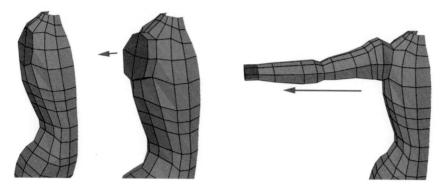

Select the polygons you just modified and extrude the base of the arm. **Keep extruding** and reshaping to get the arm. As with the knee, be sure to give enough detail around the elbow to allow it to deform properly.

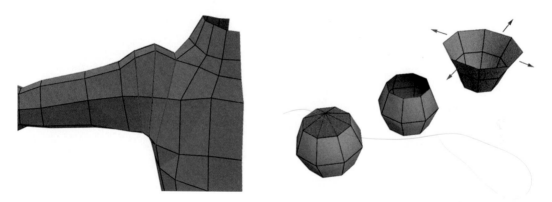

The shoulder is another critical area. Be sure the top of the shoulder is over the armpit so that the arm will deform properly. Fan-shaped detail will also help the arm deform as it rotates lower. Now we need to **create detail for the chest**. Take an eight-segment sphere and lop off the top to create a hemisphere. Reshape the remaining detail as shown.

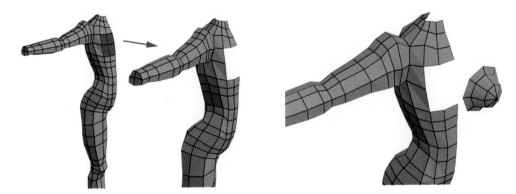

Select the polygons on the body where the chest is located and delete them. **Position the hemisphere** directly in front of this area. Because it was an eight-segment sphere, we have exactly enough detail to fit.

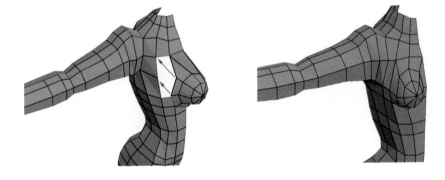

Attach or weld the corresponding vertices together. **Reshape** to match your design.

Now we need a **foot**. Start with a simple box and reshape it as shown. **Delete the four polygons** along the top and extrude the edge to make the ankle.

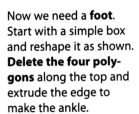

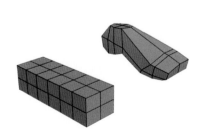

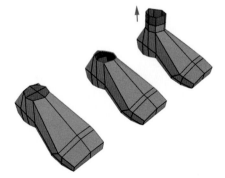

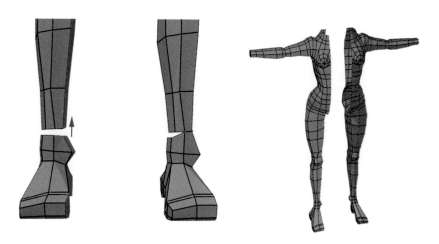

Attach the foot to the bottom of the leg. **The right half of the body** is almost complete. Duplicate it and mirror it to make the left side. Attach or weld the two sides together.

The body is complete. You can continue to model and tweak as needed.

Modeling a Hand

The hand is one of the most complex structures on the body. Each finger has three joints, and the thumb and palm are also very flexible. Here is an easy way to model a fairly flexible hand.

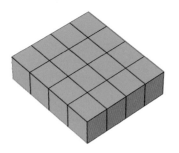 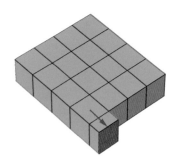 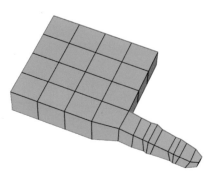

Start with a box. The number of divisions is important, because it will determine the number of fingers on the hand. In this case, we want a four-fingered hand, so we make sure there are four polygons along the front side of the box. **Select the first** of these four polygons and extrude it to create the base of the index finger. **Continue extruding** and then reshape the finger.

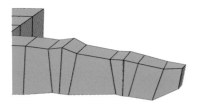 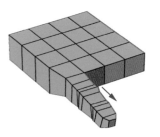 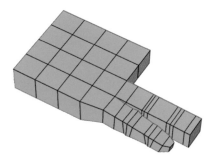

Here is a **close-up of the joints**. As you can see, the detail around the knuckles fans out slightly to assist in deformation. **Select the next polygon** along the front of the finger and extrude that. **Reshape this** to create the next finger. Another method would be to copy the index finger and attach or weld it to the appropriate place on the hand.

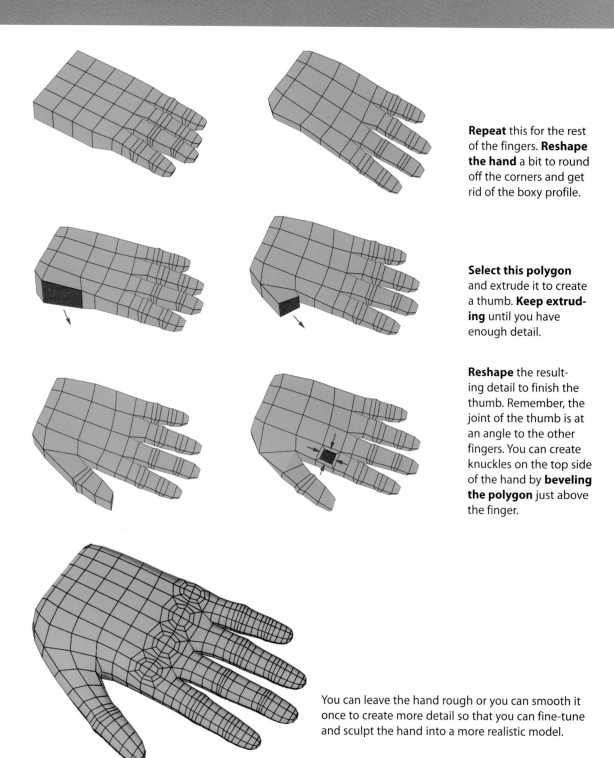

Repeat this for the rest of the fingers. **Reshape the hand** a bit to round off the corners and get rid of the boxy profile.

Select this polygon and extrude it to create a thumb. **Keep extruding** until you have enough detail.

Reshape the resulting detail to finish the thumb. Remember, the joint of the thumb is at an angle to the other fingers. You can create knuckles on the top side of the hand by **beveling the polygon** just above the finger.

You can leave the hand rough or you can smooth it once to create more detail so that you can fine-tune and sculpt the hand into a more realistic model.

Facial Modeling

To build digital heads and faces, you need to understand the underlying anatomy of the human head and face. The face is by far the most important part of the equation, since this is where most of the movement takes place.

The head is essentially made of two large bones—the skull and the jaw. The skull is really a collection of many smaller bones stitched together by cartilage, but you can think of it as a single mass balanced on the top of the spine. The jaw is the second major bone. Its movement affects the shape of the lower part of the face. When the mouth opens, the jaw's rotation does all the work. Though we don't see the skull and jaw, their influence defines the structure and movement of the face and muscles that cover it.

The Muscles of the Face

The face is a complex collection of muscles that pull and stretch the skin in a variety of ways. Knowledge of these muscles and their functions will help guide the construction of your character's head and face. Let's take a look at these muscle groups.

The head consists of two large masses—the skull and the jaw.

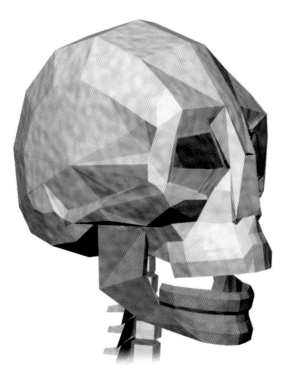

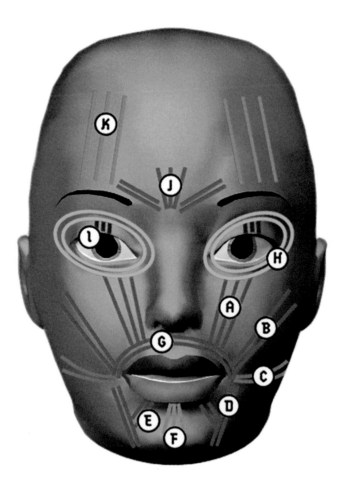

A. Levator labii superioris—This muscle runs along the side of the nose and connects to the middle of the top lip. Used alone, it will pull the top lip up into a sneer.

B. Zygomatic major—This muscle lies across the cheek and connects to the corner of the mouth. Used alone, it will pull the mouth into a smile.

C. Risorius—This muscle stretches over the jaw and attaches at the corner of the mouth. Used alone, it pulls the mouth to the side and down, as when crying.

D. Triangularis—This muscle stretches over the lower side of the jaw and pulls the corner of the mouth down. It is used when frowning or scowling.

E. Depressor labii inferioris—This muscle connects the lower lip to the chin. It pulls the lower lip straight down, as when speaking.

F. Mentalis—This muscle connects to the skin of the chin. When contracted, it pulls the chin up, forcing the lower lip into a pout.

G. Orbicularis oris—This muscle is attached to the corners of the mouth. It purses or tightens the lips.

H. Orbicularis oculi—This muscle connects the cheek to the inner eye area. Contraction of this muscle results in squinting.

I. Levator palpebrae—This muscle attaches to the upper eyelid and raises it when surprised.

J. Corrugator—This muscle runs from the bridge of the nose to the middle of the eyebrow. It pulls the eyebrows down and in, as when frowning or concerned.

K. Frontalis—This muscle runs across the forehead and connects to the eyebrows. It pulls the eyebrows up.

The Flexibility of the Face

All of this anatomy is great, but how does it affect the way a digital model is created and animated? The trick is to understand how these muscles pull and shape the face to create expressions. The groups of muscles fall into two categories: lower-face muscles that control the mouth and jaw and upper-face muscles that control the eyes and brows.

If we can create a digital model of a face that moves easily along the same lines that these muscles are pulling, we can animate the face more convincingly.

The muscles surrounding the mouth pull the skin radially outward and also allow the lips to pucker. When being modeled, the mouth also needs the detail to be arranged radially. This gives the mouth maximum flexibility and makes deformation look natural. Similarly, the **eyes** should also have radial detail. This allows the eyes not only to open and close, but also to widen and narrow.

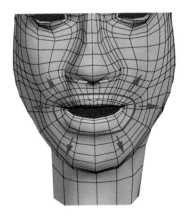

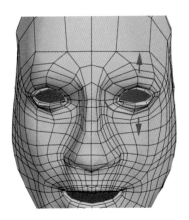

At the brows, the frontalis muscles raise and lower the eyebrows. The corrugator pulls the eyebrows in toward the bridge of the nose, furrowing the brow.

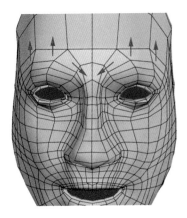

Modeling a Simple Head

Now that we understand where the detail on the face needs to be arranged, we can start modeling. The first head will be a stylized one, using box modeling techniques. This head looks similar to a clay or stop-motion puppet, but it will be fairly easy to model and animate.

Start with a **cube**. **Subdivide or smooth** the box twice. This will round off the edges so the box becomes spherical, and it will also add enough detail to create the model. **Start by modeling the mouth.** Select these faces toward the bottom of the front side of the model. Bevel them to get the required radial detail. In this case, we're adding one loop of extra detail, but you can add more later, if needed.

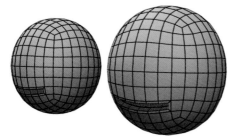  

Select the faces at the center of the bevel and extrude them into the head to create a mouth cavity. **Reshape the detail** surrounding the cavity to make a basic mouth shape. Now let's move on to the **eyes**. Select the vertices surrounding these faces and round off the edges to create a rounder eye-socket shape.

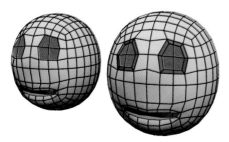

As we did with the mouth, **bevel these polygons** to get more radial detail. Now **extrude these polygons** into the head to create basic eye sockets.

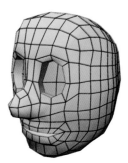

Select these polygons along the front of the face and extrude to make a nose. A character with a longer or more complex nose may require more detail. **Reshape this detail** into a basic nose. Now we have the basic parts of the head in place, and we can **start sculpting the character's head** in greater detail. Reshape the head to match your character's design. If you're using drawings as a reference, match your profile and front views.

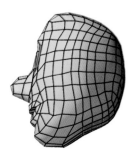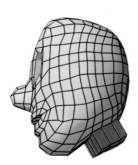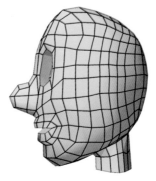

Once you're happy with the shape, **select some vertices** on the bottom of the head and extrude a neck. **Reshape the neck** to match your design.

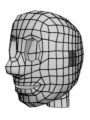
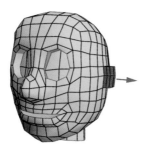

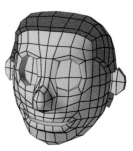

This character has very **stylized ears**, which can be created by extruding some polygons on the side of the head and reshaping them. We can also create some **stylized hair** by selecting the polygons along the top, side, and back of the head and extruding a simple hairstyle.

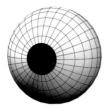
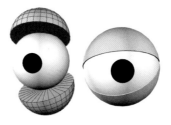

Now it's on to the **eyes**. Most characters will use a simple sphere for an eye, and this one is no exception. This particular character will **use simple hemispheres for the eyelids**. These are just slightly bigger than the spheres used for the eyeballs and fit right over them.

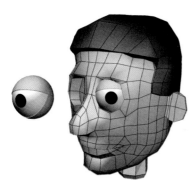
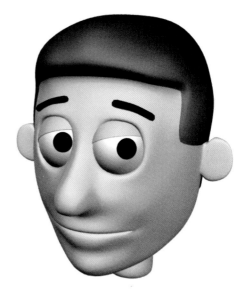

The eyes are then fit into the sockets. If you want, you could add a little more detail to the eye sockets and model a lid that is part of the surface of the face. Finally, **add some separate eyebrows** to complete the head.

Modeling a Realistic Human Head

This head is a little more complex than the previous one but is also much more accurate. It can be the basis of a very realistic character, or it can be reshaped into something more stylized.

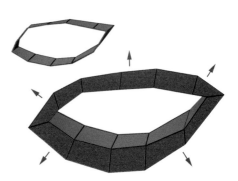

Start with a simple, open-ended cylinder. This will become the eye socket. This particular cylinder has 11 sides. **Reshape this** to create a basic eye outline. **Select the edges** along the front side of the eye socket, and extrude them.

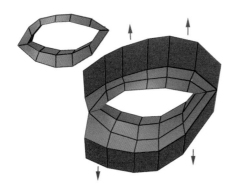
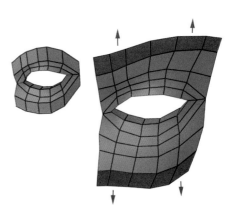

Select the top row of edges and extrude them up, then extrude down the bottom row of edges. This will create the rest of the eye. **Continue extruding** to make the cheek and forehead.

Now create a mouth. As with the eye, begin by creating an open-ended cylinder, this time with 22 divisions. **Reshape the cylinder** to create a basic mouth opening. As you did with the eye, **extrude the forward edges** of the mouth opening to create more detail.

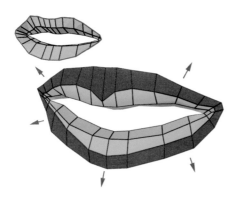 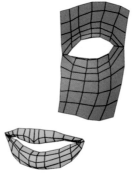

Continue extruding and reshaping to make the mouth. Now we need to **join the upper lip to the cheek**. Position the mouth next to the cheek.

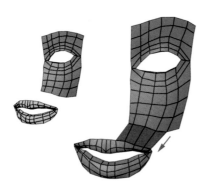 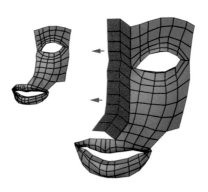

Create new polygons to fill the gap. **Now for the nose.** Select the edges along the side of the nose and extrude them.

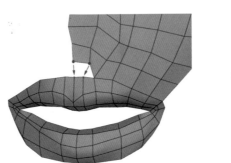

Weld or attach the bottom vertices of the nose to the top of the lip. Let's **model the rest of this in halves** to save time. Select the free side of the mouth and delete it.

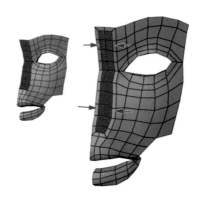
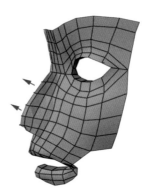

This nose will need more detail. Bevel or inset these polygons to create that detail. **Start pulling out the nose** to create the desired profile.

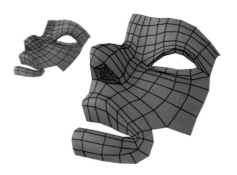

Select these polygons on the underside of the nose and extrude them inward to create a nostril. **Select the remaining edges** along the underside of the mouth and extrude them.

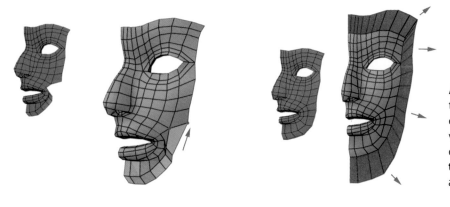

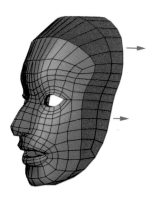

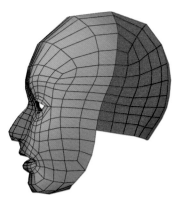

Attach or weld the vertices on the upper edge of this new detail to the vertices on the underside of the cheek. **Extrude the edges** of the face to add more detail.

Resculpt to create a fairly complete face mask. **Duplicate and mirror** this object to create the opposite side of the face. Join the two sides together.

Extrude more edges to create enough detail for the chin and the top of the forehead. **Extrude the edges** along the top of the head and rotate the detail around to create the back of the skull. Keep extruding to finish the back of the head.

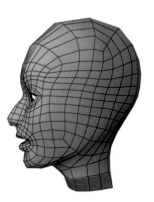

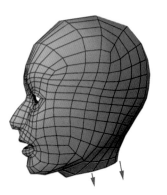

Select the detail under the head and extrude to create a neck. **Finish reshaping** the neck.

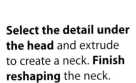

The head is complete.

Final Assembly

Once you have modeled all of the basic body parts, it's time to assemble your character. If your character was designed in segments, all you will need to do is scale the parts and place them together in preparation for rigging.

Seamless characters take a bit more work to assemble, because the various parts need to be attached using modeling tools. When assembling a character in this way, you may run across spots where the detail doesn't exactly line up. If this happens, you can do a little remodeling or tuck the rough spots into places where nobody will see them, such as under the hair at the back of the neck.

This character was built so that the seams at the collar, wrists, and ankles are hidden under clothing, making assembly easy.

The final character is ready for rigging.

Final assembly for this seamless character starts by positioning and scaling the parts.

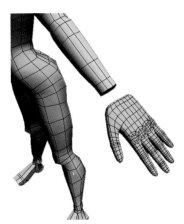

Start the process with the hands, attaching them at the wrists.

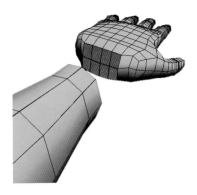

The forearm has eight vertices around its circumference. That means we need to find the same number of vertices on the hand. Select these polygons.

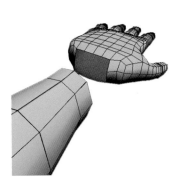

Delete them to create a hole.

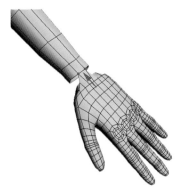

Start welding or attaching the vertices on the hand to the corresponding vertices on the forearm. Work your way around.

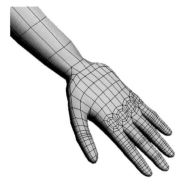

The hand is attached. Repeat on the other side.

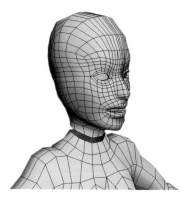

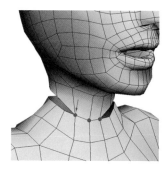

The process is very similar for the **head**. Position it above the collar. **Start welding** or attaching the vertices and work your way around.

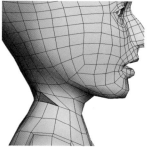

This particular character had a **slight difference in the number of vertices** between the head and body. The discrepancy is hidden toward the back of the neck, where it won't be seen. **The character is complete.** Add some texture (and maybe some hair) and it's ready for rigging.

Conclusion

By following these tutorials, you should have gained a good understanding of how to properly model characters for animation. Take some time and use these techniques to model a character of your own. As you model, pay attention to how the character is constructed, and make sure that it will deform smoothly. Once you've modeled a character, the next step is to rig it, which sets up the character with a skeleton and other controls so that it can be animated with ease.

CHAPTER THREE

Rigging Characters

Once your character is modeled, you'll need to get it ready for animation. This process is called rigging. The goal of rigging is to add a skeleton and controls to your model so that an animator can manipulate and animate the character. A properly built skeleton can be quickly and easily manipulated to attain any pose. Once the skeleton is built, it can deform the character in a way that will, ideally, make the rendered character look alive to the audience.

A good character rigger is part animator, part programmer, and part interface designer. The rigger needs to understand how animators work and translate that into an efficient setup. The perfect setup allows animators to have as much control over the character as they need while automatically managing the parts of a character that animators don't have to think about.

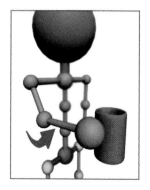  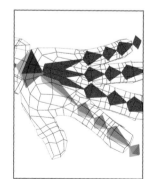 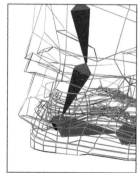

Hierarchies and Character Animation

Most 3D packages organize information about your character into a hierarchy. Essentially, the hierarchy tells the computer that the foot bone's connected to the shin bone, the shin bone's connected to the thigh bone, and so on. The hierarchy looks a bit like a tree, with each connection forming a branch. It's very similar to the nested directories found on your computer. Once you've chosen a means of animating your character, you can make a decision about how to set up the hierarchy.

A hierarchy tells the computer in what order the character's parts should be assembled.

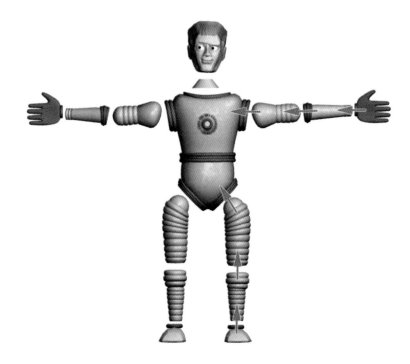

A hierarchy can be represented as a tree or a graph.

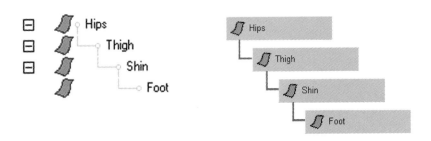

The root of a character's body is almost always the hips or pelvis. The pelvis is close to the center of gravity of the human body, which makes it a good candidate. More importantly, it is the center of weight distribution for the entire body. The pelvis supports the spine and the entire upper body, passing this weight down through the legs to the ground. Finally, almost all motions in a character start with the hips—yet another reason to have them as the root of your character's hierarchy.

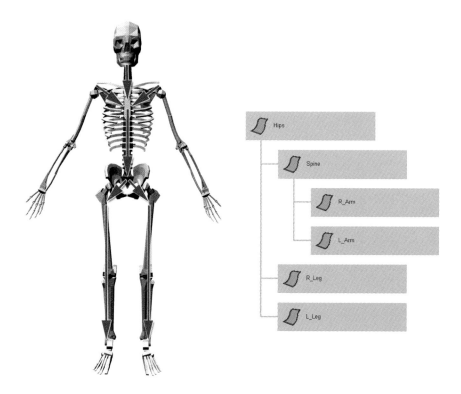

The weight of the upper body is distributed through the pelvis, where it passes through the legs to the ground. The hierarchy of a character should be centered on the hips.

Skeletons

Most single-skin characters are deformed using a skeleton made up of bones and joints. As with the human skeleton, the rigid bones are connected by joints. In most 3D packages, bones are helper objects that don't render. They sit inside the skin of a character and act as a guide for the deformation utility that actually deforms the mesh of the character.

There are differences, however, between real bones and the virtual bones in a 3D application. Virtual bones exist simply to help the skeleton deform a mesh. They may not have to match a real skeleton exactly. The few dozen bones in the spine, for example, can usually be represented by a handful of virtual bones. There may also be places in a virtual skeleton where additional bones are required to help deform the mesh properly.

A skeleton made of bones fits into the character's mesh.

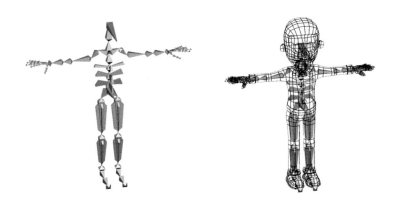

When the skeleton is animated, the character's mesh deforms to match.

To build a skeleton, you'll place the bones within the mesh and then assemble them into a hierarchy that can be animated. Once a skeleton is assembled, there are two strategies for manipulating and animating a skeleton: forward kinematics and inverse kinematics.

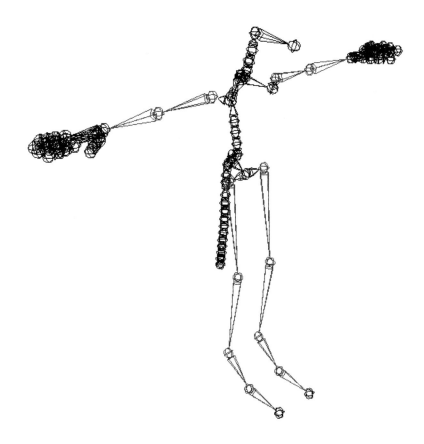

Software packages display bones and skeletons in a variety of ways, but many use simple tetrahedral shapes that do not render.

Forward Kinematics

Forward kinematics (FK) is the default method for manipulating hierarchies or skeletons. It is rotation based, which means that you position the joints by rotating them around each other. This is essentially the way human joints actually work, and it provides a good simulation of reality.

If, for example, you want to place a character's hand on a coffee cup, you first rotate the shoulder, then the elbow, then the wrist and fingers, working your way from the top of the hierarchy on down. Each rotation brings the hand closer to the cup.

Since forward kinematics is rotation based, you can't simply pick up the hand and place it on the cup. This would merely move the hand to the cup, leaving the wrist behind.

To move the hand to the cup using forward kinematics, first rotate the shoulder, then the elbow, and so on until the hand reaches the cup.

Inverse Kinematics

Inverse kinematics (IK) works the opposite way; it's translation based instead of rotation based. Inverse kinematics is easy to use: you place the character's hand on the coffee cup, and the rest of the arm automatically follows. This simple action is more complex than you might think, because the software must solve the rotations for all of the joints in the arm so that the bones remain connected to each other and look natural.

To make things more complicated, there can be many ways of orienting a character's arm so that the hand rests on the cup. The computer doesn't know how the joints of the body are supposed to move—if it's just as easy to bend the elbow backward or sideways to make the arm meet the cup, that's fine with the computer. This problem can be resolved to some degree by using parameters such as rotation limits, but IK can still be unpredictable, particularly when used on limbs with a large range of motion, like arms.

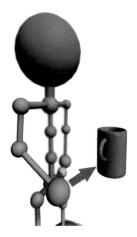

To move the hand to the cup using inverse kinematics, simply grab the hand and move it to the cup.

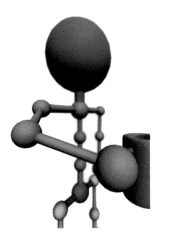 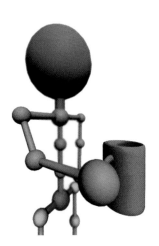 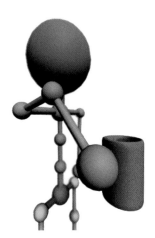

The one problem with inverse kinematics is that there can be more than one solution to the problem. Here, the arm can take several positions and the hand will still reach the cup.

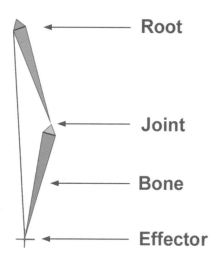

Root

Joint

Bone

Effector

The parts of an IK chain include the root, joint, bone, and effector.

The Parts of an IK Chain

An IK chain consists of a group of joints whose rotations are manipulated by an object called an effector. The first joint in an IK chain is known as the root of the chain. It's also the root of the hierarchy, but may not be the root of the entire skeleton. This joint may also contain data that helps position the chain, depending on the software. Moving the root of the IK chain moves everything below it in the hierarchy.

The tip of the last joint of the chain is called the effector. This element controls the position of the end of the IK chain. The software will always try to position the chain so that it runs between the root and the effector.

Bones (connected by joints) lie between the root and the effector and act as articulated points in the chain. An arm would have one joint—the elbow—while a spine may have many joints.

Manipulating a Chain

You manipulate the IK chain using the effector. As you move the effector, the joints of the chain rotate accordingly. This makes posing and animating a character easy, because you need to consider the position of only a single effector, rather than the rotation of many joints.

What happens when you pull the effector beyond the limits of the joints? Most software keeps the joints at a fixed length, so the fully extended chain simply aims itself at the effector. Some software, however, can allow the joints to stretch, expanding the length of the entire chain to meet the effector. This sort of effect can be used for cartoony squashing and stretching motions.

At the other end of the chain, translating the root typically moves the entire chain. If the IK effector is outside of this hierarchy, the end of the chain will stay locked to the world. The effector can also be connected to another object via hierarchies, or to a constraint to make the joints follow another object. If a character is riding a bike, for example, effectors at the hands can keep the arms locked to the bike's handlebars.

Joint Limits

To prevent joints from bending the wrong way, you may need to inform the software exactly what the limits are for a specific joint. Most packages allow for these limits to be configured on a joint-by-joint and axis-by-axis basis. Some packages have different types of joints and let you specify a joint as either hinged (two-dimensional) or ball and socket (three-dimensional).

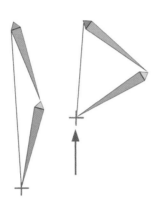

Translating the effector bends the IK chain.

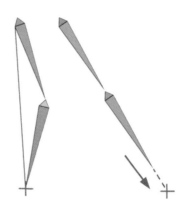

When the effector is moved beyond the limits of the chain, the chain simply aims itself at the effector.

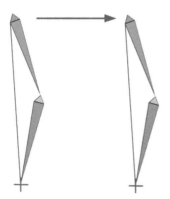

Moving the topmost bone of the chain moves the entire chain.

If the effector is outside of the hierarchy, however, as in this figure, the end of the chain stays in place.

Rest Positions and Goals

Many packages have incorporated the idea of a default joint position, also known as a rest or goal position, for a series of skeleton joints. Setting a default position forces the chain to return to the default shape when the effector is moved to its default position. The default position is usually the one in which the joints were originally created, but some packages allow for it to be redefined at any time.

This feature helps animation considerably because it makes the behavior of the skeleton quite predictable. It is also exceptionally good for chains with many joints, like an animal's tail.

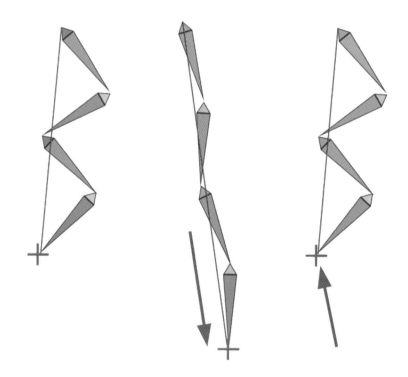

A rest position tries to keep the IK chain in the same shape when the effector is moved.

Controlling IK Chain Direction

You'll also need to consider the overall direction of the chain itself. The knees are a good example: a character's knees can point either straight ahead or out to the sides. Both of these solutions are acceptable, but manipulating that angle requires some extra control. Depending on the software, several methods can be used to specify how the joint should bend. The angle is often a separate attribute that can be modified or animated. Another method is to create a constraint in the form of a helper object. Under this method, the knee would point at this helper object, and you would animate the object to control the angle of the knee.

Mixing Forward and Inverse Kinematics

While IK is almost always used for legs, it's not always the best option for other parts of the body. Since forward kinematics is based on rotations, its default motion causes the joints to move along rotational arcs, which looks more natural because it is the way real skeletons work. This is much more desirable than IK's default motion, which is a straight line. Of course, there are many times when you will need IK to lock down the hands, but when the hands are free, FK can be much easier to animate.

In order to meet these differing needs, most advanced packages offer some method of switching between FK and IK, often by letting you change the influence of the IK effector. When it's at 100 percent, IK is fully engaged; change that influence to zero and FK is fully engaged.

An IK solution for the legs can have the knees point forward or out to the sides.

You can make animation easier by having the knee point to a helper object.

[TUTORIAL]

Building a Skeleton

Building a skeleton is much the same as putting together a segmented character. In the next two exercises, you will build a skeleton for a body and for a hand.

Start with the model of your character. In the side viewport, **draw two bones** for the upper and lower leg. Be sure to center the bones within the leg, with the knee placed properly. These bones will be an IK chain. **Duplicate these bones** to make the opposite leg, and position the new bones. Give the leg bones meaningful names.

Now **make a bone to represent the pelvis**, centered at the base of the spine. It's a good idea to make this bone protrude through the character's belly, because it'll be easier to select. **Now create two hip bones** that connect the tops of the legs to the pelvis. The hierarchy of these bones should be similar to that of the graph on the right.

 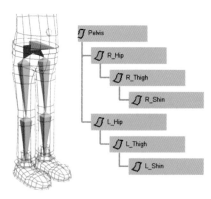

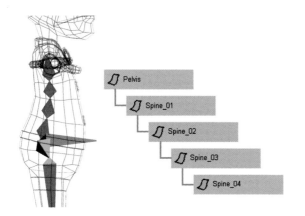

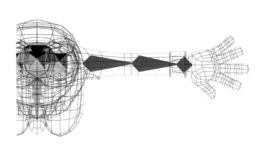

Now create a spine, being sure to place the bones along the back of the character. The number of bones you use will depend on the character. In this case we're
using four bones. Make this chain a child of the pelvis. Next, **draw the bones** for
the arm. Be sure to keep them centered and to position the elbow properly.

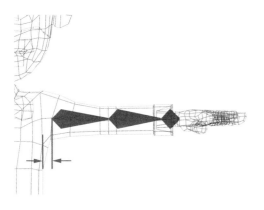

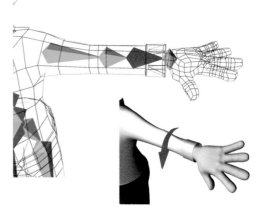

The shoulder joint is best placed over the armpit and
slightly to the side of the torso, to give enough clear-
ance for the arm to rotate to the side.

Another common way to create the arm is to **add a
third bone** in the forearm to simulate the twisting of
the radius and ulna.

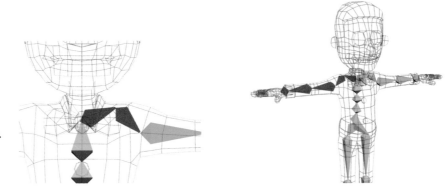

Next, **create a clavicle and shoulder bone** to join the arm to the spine. Then **duplicate the arm** and position it on the other side.

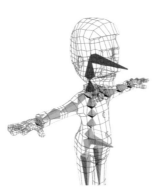
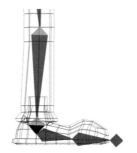

Add a few neck bones and a head bone to the top of the spine. Like the pelvis bone, the head bone can protrude slightly from the mesh to make selection easier. **Create two bone**s to make a foot. **Duplicate them** to make the other side, and position them accordingly.

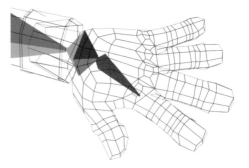

The main skeleton is now complete, except for the hands. **Start the hand skeleton** by drawing a bone from the wrist to the knuckle of the index finger.

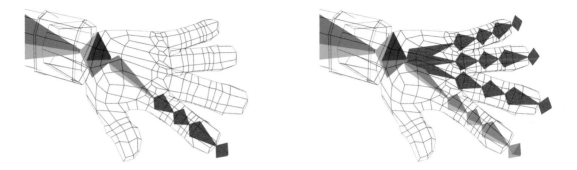

Continue drawing to make a bone for each joint in the index finger. **Repeat this process** for the other fingers.

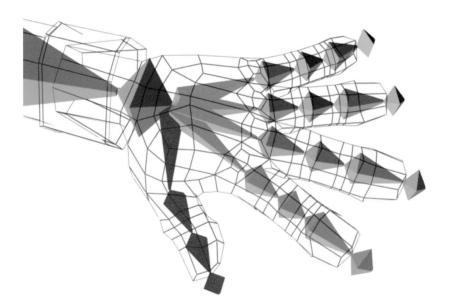

Finish up by creating bones for the thumb. Duplicate and mirror this mesh to create the skeleton for the other hand.

Facial Rigging

The face is a very complex surface that can assume a huge variety of shapes. Facial animation is probably the most difficult task an animator faces, and having a good rig will help the process along considerably.

While tools such as wire deformers, bones, and clusters have been used for facial animation, the most popular method by far is a process called morphing, which allows one object to assume the shape of another. Since the face is so complicated, it is best to sculpt the individual poses a character's face may take. This allows for precise control of the specific shapes. A morphing utility will allow you to smoothly animate between these shapes.

Multiple-target morphing lets you mix and blend multiple shapes to create new shapes. In facial animation, this provides even greater control over the shape of the face, because it allows you to mix and blend shapes representing the extremes in any ratio or combination.

Morphing allows you to take two or more shapes and combine them.

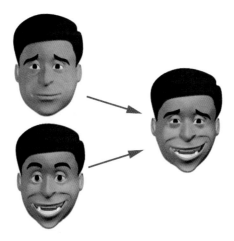

Most 3D packages provide a slider-based interface to control the weights of the individual morphs.

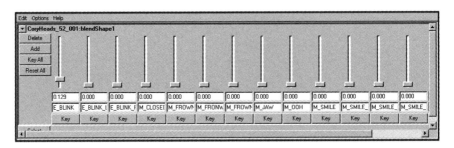

Modeling Morph Targets for Animation

The best way to model morph targets for animation is to study the underlying anatomy of the face. Since each muscle is connected to the face in a specific place, flexing just that muscle will change the shape of only part of the face. If you model the exact shape that one muscle would create when tensed, you will have an anatomically correct animation, once all of the shapes and hence all of the muscles are mixed together.

Ideally, you could model targets for every single muscle in the face, which amounts to several dozen targets. For ease of use, this book will outline a dozen or so of the most useful shapes. While some of these poses combine several muscles, the theory is the same: each slider controls only part of the face. ("Slider" is a generic term for an object or interface element that, when manipulated, controls another object.)

When modeling for a morph system, be careful to move only those vertices that need to be affected by any particular muscle. If, for example, you accidentally move a vertex on the ear while working on a mouth motion, the character's ear may change shape every time the jaw opens. Also be sure to make smooth transitions from the right to left sides of the face. When you model a right-side smile, make sure that the smile transitions smoothly to the left side of the face, and vice versa. If the same part of the face is manipulated by more than one slider, you may get unwanted results, like a top lip that goes bonkers when both smile sliders are moved.

These target poses are extremes, so try to model the biggest smile, the saddest frown, and so on. Try looking in the mirror and using your own face as a reference.

Basic Facial Poses

For almost any character, you'll need to model a number of basic facial poses. These poses are fundamental to proper facial animation and are based on the motion of the major muscles of the face. In addition to the basic poses, you can create additional poses to help speed animation.

Lower-Face Poses

Lower-face poses are centered on the mouth, though some, such as the smile and sneer, affect the eyes a bit. Lower-face poses are usually used for lip sync but can also be a part of many other expressions.

This first pose is the **open jaw**. Model it by selecting the vertices of the lower face and then moving them down and slightly back to simulate the effect of the jaw rotating open. The **pursed lip**, or "oooh" shape is the product of the orbicularis oris muscle. When you model this shape, be sure to maintain volume in the lips, which get slightly thicker as the muscle contracts.

Smiles are primarily the action of the zygomatic major muscle. In a smile, the corner of the mouth is pulled up into the cheek, which creates a smile line and expands the volume of the cheek.

This frown is a combination of the triangularis and depressor labii inferioris muscles. These muscles pull the corner of the mouth down.

The depressor anguli oris muscle pulls the mouth out to express disgust or fear. When tightened, this muscle can also affect the tendons in the neck. Again, separating this into right and left will give you more options when animating.

The sneer is the product of the levator labii superioris muscle. It pulls the lip up toward the edge of the nose. It also affects the skin along the side of the nose all the way up to the corner of the eye.

Upper-Face Poses

While many animators concentrate on the mouth and lip sync, true emotion is communicated through the eyes, brows, and upper face. Good upper-face animation is critical to any facial animation.

The corrugator pulls the brow down and in toward the bridge of the nose. In an extreme position, the character looks angry, though this shape is also used for many other emotions.

The left and right eyebrows are lifted by the frontalis. Model each brow separately to achieve maximum control.

Another pose to model is worry, with the brow furrowed and the eyebrows down.

For the eyes, blinks are always important.

Creating an extra pose for the lower lids can help with squinting and other actions.

It also helps to make a pose in which the eyes widen.

Other Facial Poses

You can create all sorts of other poses to get very specific expressions. You'd usually create these poses as needed and for specific scenes or situations.

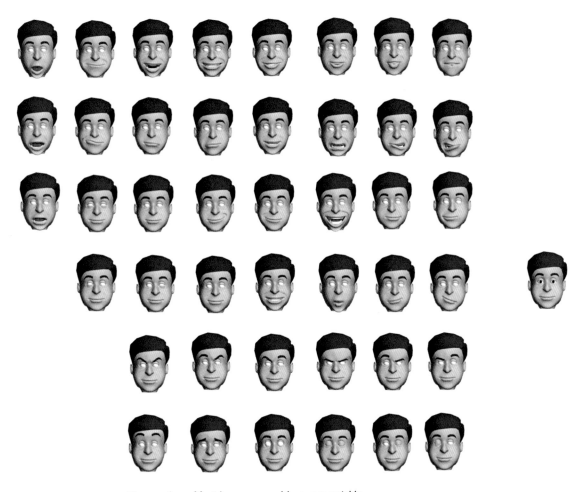

The number of facial poses can add up very quickly.

Mesh Deformation

Once you've built the skeleton and fitted it to a mesh, you can use it to deform the skin of your character. You can do this using a technique called mesh deformation, also known as "skinning" or "binding," which uses the position of the bones to determine the shape of the mesh. As you move the bones of the skeleton, the skin of the character deforms to match.

The goal of any mesh deformation utility is to move vertices. Each vertex in the character's mesh is assigned to follow one or many bones. When a bone moves, the vertices follow and maintain their relative distance to the bone. The vertices of the thigh need to follow the thighbone, for example, while both the upper and lower leg will affect the vertices around the knee. When more than one bone affects a vertex, their influence must be weighted.

A weighted deformation allows more than one bone to affect a given vertex. The method of accomplishing this depends on the software you use, but the underlying theory is the same for all packages. Each bone affects each vertex, using a weight from 0 to 1. When the weight is at 0, the vertex is unaffected by the bone. When the weight is at 1, the bone completely controls the motion of the vertex, and the vertex is said to be fully affected. Weights in the middle of the range allow multiple bones to affect a vertex.

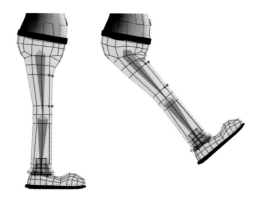

In a mesh deformation system, the vertices follow the motion of the bones.

Vertices near the joints are weighted so they're affected by both bones.

You can set up weighting using a combination of methods, which include envelopes, painted weights, and numerical assignment. Each of these methods accomplishes the same goal: assigning weights to vertices so that they will follow the bones.

Envelopes

Envelopes are probably the most common way to set up weighting. An envelope is essentially a range of influence that surrounds the bone. This range of influence is typically displayed as a capsule shape that you can move and resize to match the character's mesh. When envelopes overlap, the vertices in the overlapping areas are weighted accordingly. Envelopes can also have what is known as a falloff range, which reduces the strength of the envelope to zero over a user-specified distance. Use of a falloff range helps create smooth transitions between bones.

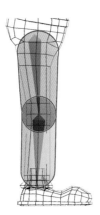

An envelope surrounds a bone and affects all the vertices within the envelope. When envelopes overlap at the joints, the vertices are weighted accordingly.

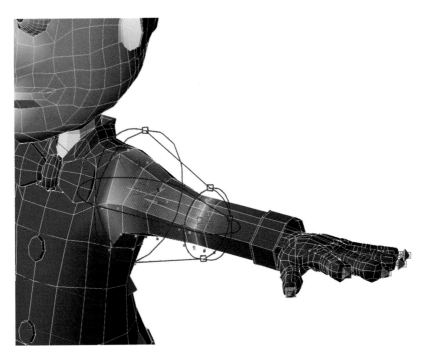

Many packages provide visual feedback to help with adjusting the envelope. In this case, the red vertices are fully affected, while the yellow ones are weighted.

Painted Weights

Some packages, such as Maya, allow you to use 3D painting tools to generate weight maps. This gives you more control in tricky areas because weights can more closely fit the shape of the character than a capsule-shaped envelope can. When combined with a pressure-sensitive tablet, it can be a very effective way to skin a character.

Numerical Assignment

Most advanced packages have some sort of interface that allows you to type in the weights for each vertex. This gives you tons of control, but you'd usually use it only to tweak trouble spots, because typing in weight values for every vertex in a character would be a long, tedious process.

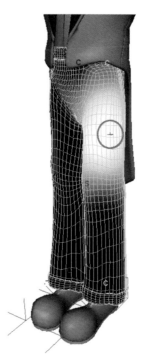

Painted weights allow you to use a brush to assign vertex weights interactively.

Polygons	AdvPolygons	Weighted Deformers	Rigid Skins	Smooth Skins	Springs	Particles				
	lAnkle	lBallFoot	lHip	lKnee	rAnkle	rBallFoot	rHip	rKnee		
Hold	off	off	off	off	off	off	off	off		
PANTSShape										
vtx[99]	0.000	0.000	0.431	0.569	0.000	0.000	0.000	0.000		
vtx[365]	0.000	0.000	0.000	0.000	0.000	0.000	0.420	0.579		
vtx[730]	0.000	0.000	0.431	0.568	0.000	0.000	0.000	0.000		
vtx[941]	0.000	0.000	0.657	0.342	0.000	0.000	0.000	0.000		
vtx[942]	0.000	0.000	0.627	0.372	0.000	0.000	0.000	0.000		
vtx[1534]	0.000	0.000	0.000	0.000	0.000	0.000	0.496	0.503		
vtx[1746]	0.000	0.000	0.000	0.000	0.000	0.000	0.664	0.335		
vtx[1747]	0.000	0.000	0.000	0.000	0.000	0.000	0.615	0.384		
vtx[2383]	0.000	0.000	0.426	0.574	0.000	0.000	0.000	0.000		
vtx[2655]	0.000	0.000	0.657	0.343	0.000	0.000	0.000	0.000		
vtx[2656]	0.000	0.000	0.533	0.467	0.000	0.000	0.000	0.000		
vtx[2657]	0.000	0.000	0.538	0.462	0.000	0.000	0.000	0.000		
vtx[2658]	0.000	0.000	0.431	0.568	0.000	0.000	0.000	0.000		

| 0.0000 | 0.00 | | 1.00 |

Numerical assignment involves assigning the weights numerically a vertex at a time.

Weighting a Character

The details of the character-weighting process will depend on the software you use. The general rule of thumb is to start with broad strokes and use tools like envelopes and painted weights to get most of the vertices moving properly. After that, you should use numerical assignment to fine-tune and tweak the deformation around the joints.

Start with a character that has all of the bones placed properly within the mesh. Apply the mesh deformation tool, which will apply a default deformation. The defaults almost always need to be adjusted.

The best way to test how the default deformation works is to move the joints. Start with a leg and create a short animation that runs the leg through its range of motions.

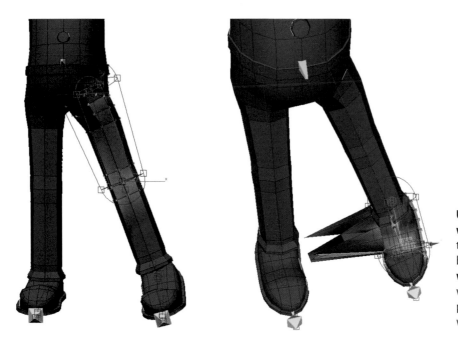

Use envelopes or weight painting to get the mesh to follow the bone. **Even very careful work** with envelopes and weight painting may still produce vertices that just won't behave.

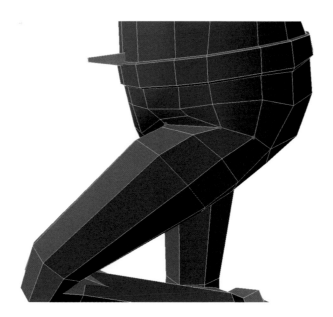

These stray vertices can be fine-tuned using numerical assignment. One place where this is usually necessary is around the hip area. By scrubbing the animation and manually changing the weights, you can work out the correct deformation.

You can then repeat these steps for the rest of the character. A good enve-lope is the result of attention to detail. Start at a high level with tools that affect a lot of vertices, then work down to the point where you refine the deformation a vertex at a time.

Test the character through a wide range of motions before you finish.

Other Deformation Tools

In addition to mesh deformation, a number of other tools can help deform a mesh. These tools can aid in skeletal or facial animation.

Clusters

Clusters are another way to animate the shape of your character. In its simplest sense, a cluster is a collection of vertices, giving you the ability to control many vertices with just one cluster. More complex systems allow you to weight vertices between one or several clusters, which can produce very subtle deformation effects on the skin of a character.

Clusters are useful in several situations: a cluster linked to a skeleton can be used as a skeletal deformation system, and you can also use clusters to simulate effects such as muscle bulging. Some people use clusters to control parts of the face in facial animation

You can also use clusters to fix trouble spots in a character; for example, you can animate a cluster to resculpt a stubborn joint on a frame-by-frame basis.

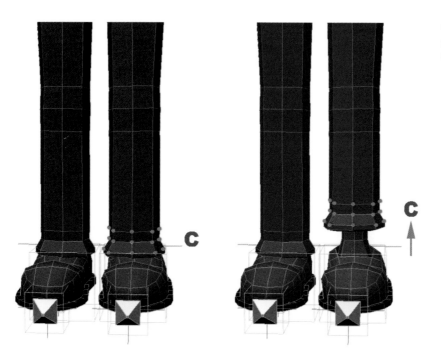

You can use a cluster to move a specific set of vertices.

Wires

While clusters use sets of points to affect a surface, wires go a step further and use simple curves to affect the surface. This gives you much broader control and is used a lot in facial animation to animate the eyebrows, or even the mouth.

Lattices

Lattices are grids of points that you can use to affect the shape of a character's skin. Most commonly, they're used to affect soft areas of the body—to add jiggle to a belly, for example. Some packages use lattices to simulate muscle bulging and control the deformation around joints.

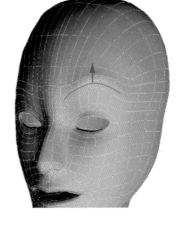

Wires are splines that can deform geometry.

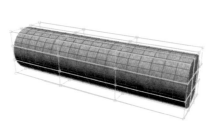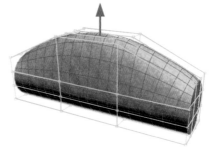

Lattices can be used to deform skin.

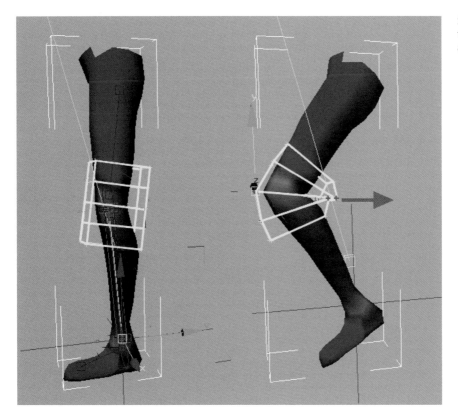

Some packages use lattices to affect deformations around joints.

Refining Rigs

One of the goals of rigging is to make animation easier. There are a number of ways to refine a character's rig to make it easy to manipulate. You can use features such as constraints to control a skeleton, and add handles and grab points to make it easy to select parts of a character.

Constraints

Constraints are a way to automatically control an object's position, scale, or orientation. You'll use constraints within a rig to do things like control the eyes or stick parts of the rig together without using hierarchies. Constraints are also useful when a character is interacting with the world: if a character lifts an object, you attach the object to the hand with a constraint.

Aim Constraints

An aim constraint constrains an object's orientation so that it points at another object in the scene. Some people use it as an alternative to inverse kinematics: you could constrain a character's wrist bone to always point at the hand, for example. Aim constraints are commonly used to control eye direction. If you constrain the eye to a helper object, the eye will always point at that object.

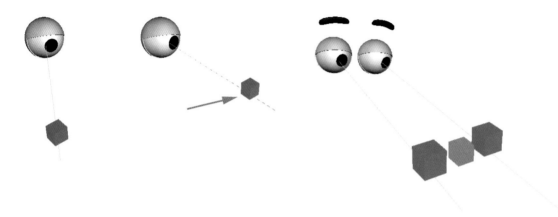

The eye is constrained to point at the helper object, using an aim constraint.

A complete eye rig involves one helper object for each eye. These are then linked hierarchically to a third object, which controls the general direction of the gaze.

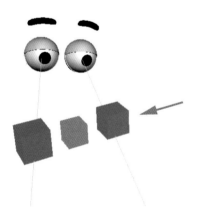

Moving the main object shifts the gaze.

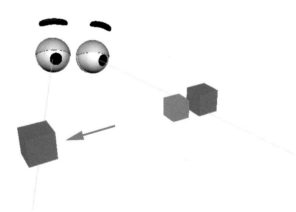

Moving an individual object changes how the eyes are angled in relation to each other.

Point Constraints

A point constraint causes one object to follow another. These are very handy when you want an object to move along with another object, but you don't want to include the second object in the hierarchy. You might also use point constraints when you want a character to lift something or when you want to attach parts of a skeleton or character together.

Vector Constraints

Another type of constraint, sometimes called a vector constraint or pole vector constraint, forces the direction of an IK chain to follow another object. Point constraints are frequently used to control the direction of the knees of the character.

Here, a point constraint is used to connect the cup to the hand.

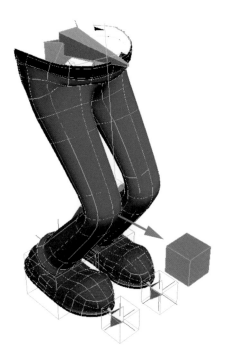

The IK chain on this character is constrained so that the knee points to a helper object. When the cube moves, the knee rotates to follow.

Grab Points and Handles

Skeletal animation is much easier when the animator can select just parts of the character. You can make parts easier to select by creating null objects that are placed as handles or grab points that the animator can use to manipulate the character. In stop-motion animation, a grab point is a hard point on a clay character that allows the animator to grab and move a joint without seriously deforming the clay. You can use grab points on digital characters as well, though in a slightly different context.

The feet and legs are a good example of areas where grab points come in handy. You could use the IK handles created by the software to manipulate the legs, but these handles are usually buried within the character's mesh and can be hard to locate. To make it easier, you can create a grab point that is outside the mesh and easy to find—and moving the grab point will, in turn, move the IK handle.

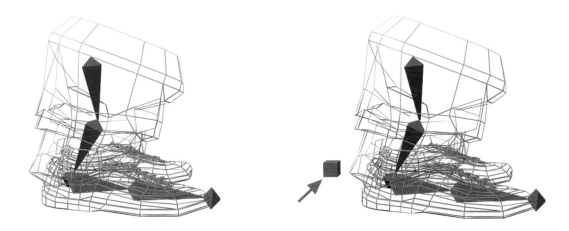

With the skeleton buried under the mesh, it's hard to see the ankle, much less select it. Creating a **grab point** outside the mesh will make selecting the ankle much easier.

Setting Up a Foot

The foot always presents problems when creating a manageable skeleton. The big problem is the way the foot rolls along the ground. The foot can pivot at any one of three points: the heel, the ball of the foot, or the toes.

Here's one way to use a series of nulls, a grab point, and a simple hierarchy to control the foot. It's been tested in 3DS Max and Maya. It involves creating three IK handles, one at the heel, one at the ball of the foot, and one at the toe.

The foot can pivot at three points.

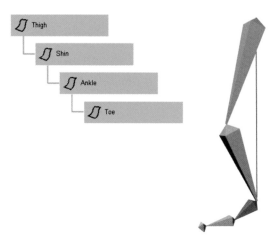

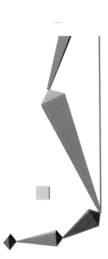

Start with a simple skeleton. The leg is a two-joint chain, while the foot bone and toe bone are single-joint chains. Make sure these are all in the same hierarchy. **Create four nulls:** one as a grab point, one at the heel, one at the ball of the foot, and one at the toe. Align the last three nulls parallel to the ground plane.

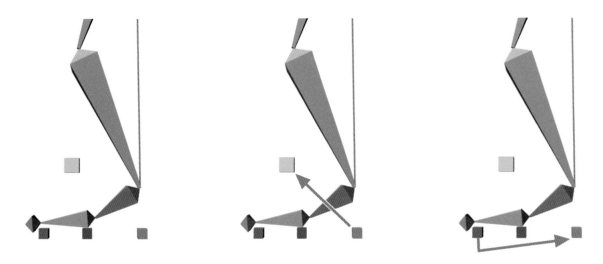

Link each IK handle to its respective null. **Make the grab point** the parent of the heel. **Make the heel** the parent of the toe.

Make the toe the parent of the ball of the foot. **That's it.** Now lifting and moving the grab point moves the foot.

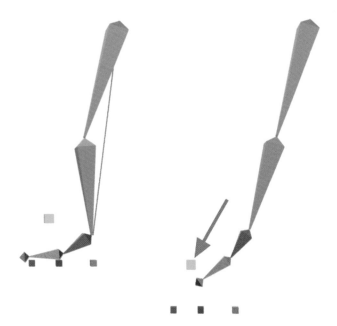

If the ankle goes beyond the IK limit, the foot naturally bends to compensate.

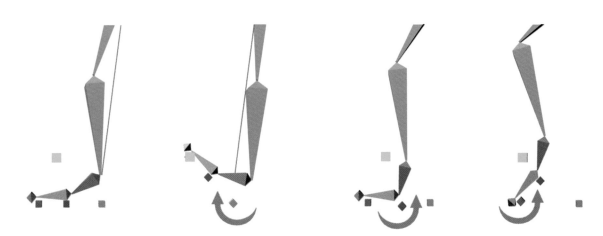

Rotating each of the other three nulls rotates the foot around each pivot point.

Refining the Foot

This rig provides a good deal of control, but you still need to select up to four different objects to manipulate the foot. This can slow down the animation in two ways. First, the animator needs to select a different object. Second, the animator needs to switch from translation to rotation in order to pivot the foot.

To improve the rig, you can create three sliders near the grab point—heel roll, ball roll, and toe roll—and then connect these attributes to the rotation of the foot. You can accomplish this in several ways, as detailed in the next section.

Sliders and Custom Attributes

Some parts of the character, like the spine and fingers, are composed of many joints that move in unison. You can simplify the animation process by connecting the motion of these objects to a single object or slider.

Many packages also allow you to create custom attributes for objects within a scene. These are variables or numerical values that you can add to an object, and they work in much the same way as a slider. These attributes, however, are not objects; they are additional attributes that are added to an existing object in the scene.

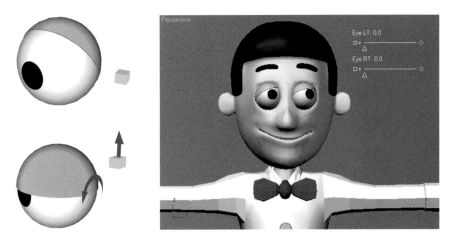

This slider is an object that controls the blink of an eye. Some packages actually supply sliders that are part of the interface, such as these sliders that also control eye blink.

One of the more common places to place attributes is in the hand. The fingers of the hand comprise almost a dozen joints, and automating these joints can save the animator a lot of grief. Since fingers tend to bend uniformly, you can tie the rotation of the three joints to one attribute. Animating that attribute bends the finger.

Simply adding a slider object or extra attributes is not enough to control another object, however. These need to be connected in some way to your character. You can connect the attributes using set-driven keys or expressions.

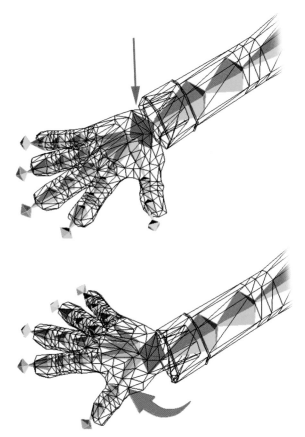

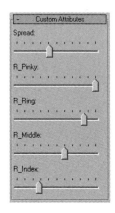

All of the controls for this hand are centered on the bone at the base of the hand. Animating the rotation of the bone rotates the hand.

This bone also has additional attributes added to it that allow you to control the bend and spread of the fingers.

Set-Driven Keys

Set-driven keys were initially developed for Alias | Wavefront's Maya, but similar techniques have appeared in other packages as well. A set-driven key expands the concept of direct relationships by allowing you to alter the relationship between objects based on a user-defined curve.

For example, if you want the eyelids of a character to stop rotating once they are closed, you could use a set-driven key to limit the rotation. A really complex use would be tying all of the joints involved in walking to a slider. Moving one slider would then move the character through the walk cycle, and adjusting the rate of the slider would vary the rate of the walk. This might not be a very practical application, but it does demonstrate the potential of this tool.

Expressions

Expressions are a way of automatically connecting parts of a scene or character. Instead of using a keyframe, you use an expression, which automatically calculates the animation data every time a new frame is encountered. Expressions can be used for the simple task of making one object follow another or for complex systems that create virtual control panels for your characters.

Expressions are powerful tools. You can use them to create complex motions that make animation much easier. You can also use them to create relationships among different parts of a character, so that when you move one part, the others follow along. Be careful with expressions, though, because you can easily overautomate a character, making it difficult to control and hard to animate in a natural-looking way.

Conclusion

Character rigging is the most technical task an animator will face. Most large studios separate out the job of rigging to free the animators for the work of bringing characters to life. Still, it's very important for animators to understand the basics of rigging and how characters are built: just as a race car driver needs to understand how his car works, the animator needs to know how a character is rigged before taking it for a spin.

CHAPTER FOUR

Basics of Animation

Once your character is modeled and rigged, you're ready to start animating. Animation is a motion-based art, and an understanding of the way objects move is very important to becoming a good animator. The laws of motion are the foundation of the science of physics, and a little knowledge of physics can go a long way toward giving your characters a sense of realism.

Motion is intimately related to time. In fact, motion is simply the change of an object's position over time. Time is a raw material that actors, comedians, and musicians use constantly. Good comic timing means knowing exactly when to spring the punchline. Good animation timing means knowing exactly when your character should react, blink, or pull that huge mallet out from behind his back. Timing is the only thing that separates animation from illustration. Developing a good sense of timing is very important to becoming a good animator.

On top of the basic physics of motion, you also have to consider the meaning of motion. A character moves his body for a reason, and these motions are very important because they convey the character's mood and personality to the audience. Only through motion can the character truly come to life.

Understanding Motion

If you've ever studied physics, you'll know that motion is the result of forces acting on an object. In order for an object to move or to change direction, a force needs to be applied. We all know about the force of gravity, which pulls objects to the ground, but there are plenty of other forces that affect the way characters move, including wind, the weight of a heavy object, or even the forces exerted by a character's own muscles. A strong character moves much differently than a weakling does.

Motion is an object's change in position over time.

When an object moves farther in the same amount of time, it has a higher velocity.

Acceleration is a change in velocity.

Deceleration is another change in velocity, but in the opposite direction.

Gravity and Other Forces

The most constant force in our world is that of gravity; if you live on Earth, or any other planet for that matter, you can't escape it. Knowing how gravity works will give you a good understanding of how all forces work.

Back in the 1600s, Isaac Newton figured out a mathematical formula to describe the effects of gravity and the laws of motion. I'm not going to bore you with equations in this book, but the basic idea is that applying a constant force to an object will cause it to accelerate. So an object subjected to the constant force of gravity will move faster and faster the longer it falls (of course, that's ignoring all other forces, such as wind resistance).

A constant force of gravity is applied to this bowling ball.

Since animation is a visual medium, let's visually depict how a force affects an object.

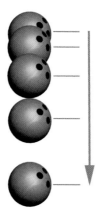

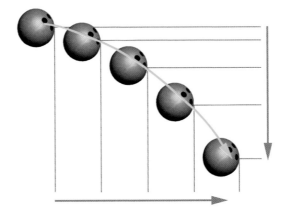

The force of gravity causes the ball to accelerate. This means that it moves farther in each frame.

When the bowling ball is tossed, the force of gravity accelerates the vertical motion in the same manner, though the horizontal motion is the same.

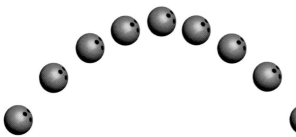

For an object tossed upward, gravity causes its upward motion to decelerate until it comes to a halt, at which point the object accelerates downward. The resulting motion traces out a parabola.

These rules apply not just for gravity, but for every other force we encounter. An automobile applies force to the ground by turning its wheels. If this force is constant, the car will accelerate and push the driver back in his seat in much the same way that gravity pulls him down.

Muscle Forces

A character's muscles also apply force. Muscles can exert a force outward, such as when lifting an object, but they also work to move the body itself. A character's muscles constantly apply force to the skeleton to keep the character standing or to make the character perform actions. These muscle forces work just the same as gravity in that they cause objects—in this case, the character's limbs—to accelerate and decelerate.

The fact that muscles apply force is a very important concept. Forces cause things to accelerate, and characters almost always accelerate into their motions and decelerate out of them. As an artist, you don't need to understand all the physics involved; you simply need to know that it takes things a while to get moving and that it also takes a while for things to stop. In animation lingo, this is known as a slow-in and slow-out.

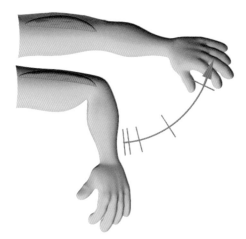

The force applied by a character's bicep bends the arm at the elbow. If this force is constant, the end of the arm accelerates as it moves.

The force applied by the triceps works in the opposite direction and decelerates the forearm, slowing it to a stop.

Momentum and Weight

For objects to appear to be real, they need to have weight. An object in a 3D application has no inherent weight. The animator is the one who gives the illusion of weight by animating that object in a specific way. The motion of the object communicates a feeling of weight to the audience.

As we have seen, the forces acting upon an object determine how the object moves. Another factor that affects how the object moves is the mass of the object itself. This is called momentum, and what it means is that the more massive an object is, the more force is needed to change that object's direction. This rule is pretty much common sense: it's much easier to stop a bicycle than it is to stop a freight train. When animating objects, you need to pay attention to this little fact of life.

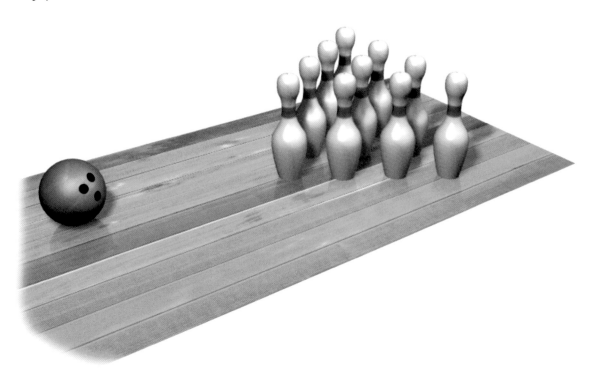

Here's a simple example. We have a ball. Is it filled with air or lead? The only way to tell is by how the ball moves.

In this example, the ball and the contents of the scene are identical. The only difference is the motion of the ball and pins. The ball's motion shows the audience the weight of the ball. Simply by changing the ball's motion, we turn it from a bowling ball into a balloon.

The ball is set in motion and rolls towards the pins.

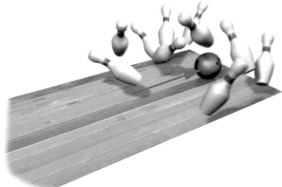

If the ball crashes through the pins, we know that it is heavy and had lots of momentum.

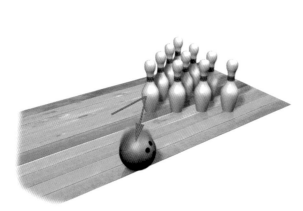

If the ball bounces off the pins, we know that it is lighter and had less momentum than the first ball.

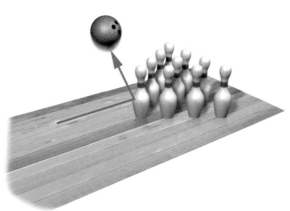

If the ball then floats upward, we see that it is filled with helium.

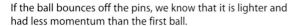

Animation Interfaces

Knowing how an object moves is important for any animator, but another essential skill is being able to create that motion within the computer. All 3D applications are slightly different, but they all use the same basic concepts to define and edit motions. These methods include setting keyframes to define the motion and editing the motions using interfaces such as the motion graph and the dope sheet.

Keyframes

In the old days of hand-drawn animation, animators would draw just the main poses of a character and let assistant animators fill in the rest. These main poses are known as keys or keyframes. In a computerized environment, the assistant animator is replaced by a computer, and a keyframe is what tells the computer where the object is at a specific time.

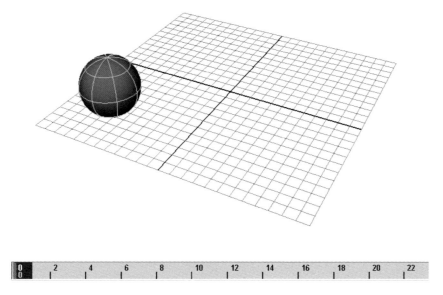

A keyframe tells the computer that the ball will be in a certain place at a certain time.

Keyframes are most typically used to define an object's position, but they can also be used to define just about any other attribute of an object, such as color, shape, or transparency. Facial animation, for example, requires key-framing an object's shape, but you also might need to keyframe the *color* of a character's cheeks if he blushes a lot.

If we add a new keyframe at a different time, we have the basics of motion. The ball has to move from point A to point B over the given period of time.

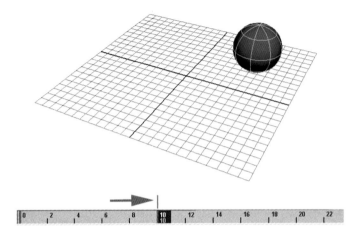

But how will the ball move between the two key-frames? We determine this by using a motion graph.

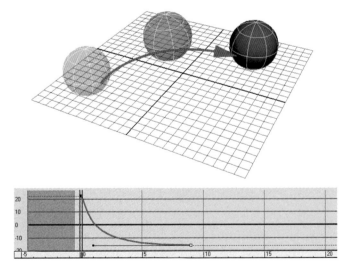

Motion Graphs

The frames between keyframe are called, appropriately enough, inbetweens. In a computer animation environment, the software calculates your inbetweens, but just as you do in traditional animation, you'll still need to tell it how to create those inbetweens. You can do this by using motion graphs, which use curves to tell the computer exactly how to move the object in between a set of keyframes. The graph itself can be anything from a straight line to a curve. Most motion graphs allow you to adjust the curve using Bézier-type handles, much like the tools used in modeling.

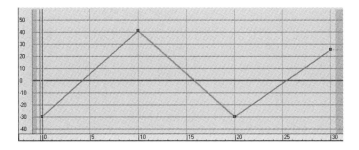

A straight line moves the object an equal amount between keyframes.

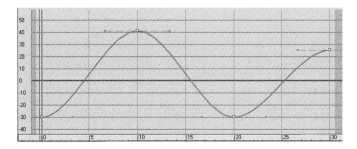

A curve can be used to slow-in and slow-out motions, creating accelerations and decelerations.

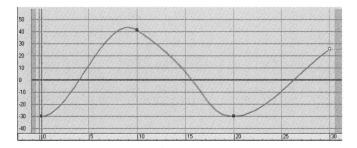

Curves can also be altered to create all sorts of custom inbetweens.

Motion graphs are an invaluable tool for the animator in diagnosing and fixing animation problems. Knowing how to read and manipulate motion graphs is an essential skill.

Every software package is different, but most motion graphs work in similar ways. Typically, the horizontal axis of the graph represents time, while the vertical axis represents the parameter being changed, such as position, rotation, scaling, and so on. These parameters are plotted graphically to tell you exactly how an object moves.

In many cases, the motion of the object will be broken down into X, Y, and Z components. While this may seem a little complicated at first, using separate curves will ultimately give you more control.

You can also use motion graphs to spot problems and tweak a character's motion. Because the motions are graphed out in a smooth curve, any interruption in this curve can signal a glitch or bump in the character's motion.

This curve has a slight "bump" at the middle keyframe, which can indicate a problem in the character's motion as well.

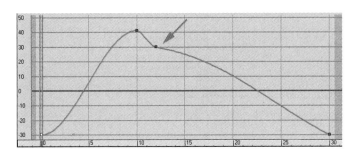

Smoothing out the curve will also smooth out the motion.

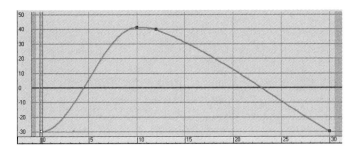

Dope Sheets

Another, simpler way to manage keyframes is by using a dope sheet. A dope sheet displays just the keyframes without the curves. Typically, the keyframes are displayed as blocks along a linear timeline, with the underlying curves hidden from view. Manipulating the keys changes the timing, but it does not affect the motion graphs; the inbetweens will follow the same curves. Since the keyframes are where you really define the motion, a simplified interface can make editing a scene much easier.

Another advantage of dope sheets is that they typically allow for higher-level editing of a character. An animator can select all the keyframes in a character's arm, for example, and reposition them to adjust the entire motion, rather than tweaking it a joint at a time.

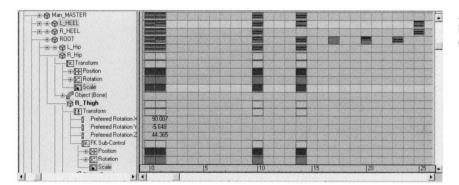

A dope sheet shows the keyframes but not the curves.

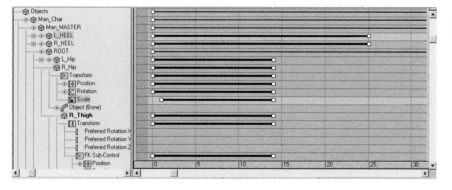

Some dope sheets allow you to move blocks of animation very quickly, allowing you to speedily retime a scene.

Trajectories

In addition to motion graphs and dope sheets, there are additional methods of viewing, but not editing, your animation within a scene. One of these ways of visualizing motion is by observing an object's trajectory. Some packages allow you to graph the motion of an object within the viewports. This is an excellent way to check the object's motion through the actual scene.

Ghosting

Ghosting is derived from classic animation and allows you to overlay multiple "exposures" of an object's motion within a viewport, much in the same way that a traditional animator views layered drawings on a light table. Ghosting can be very effective in visualizing an object's motion, particularly the motions of complex characters.

Viewing an object's trajectory in the viewport can help you determine exactly how it's moving.

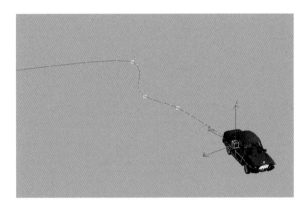

Ghosting is another way of viewing your character's motion.

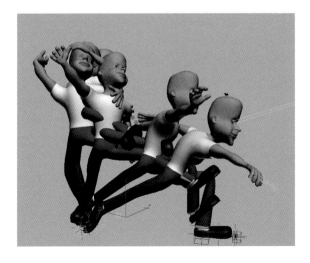

The Language of Movement

In addition to understanding the forces that affect motion and how to express those forces in a 3D software package, the animator must understand the language of movement. Animation has a very specific vocabulary of motion that animators can draw from. This vocabulary includes such things as timing, arcs, anticipation, overshoot, secondary action, follow-through, overlap, and moving holds, among others. These motions are the raw material; good timing is the glue that holds it all together.

Timing

Timing affects every aspect of a film, and on many levels. First, the film is a specific length, anything from a 30-second commercial to a two-hour feature. Second, the cutting of the scenes within this time constraint affects the mood and pace of the film. Third, the acting and timing of the character's actions affect how each individual scene plays.

Think of your film as music. Both film and music rely intimately on time. Your film's scenes can be seen as verses, choruses, or movements. The individual notes of the instruments are the same as the individual actions of your characters. Each action, like each musical note, must be in the right place at the right time. And as with music, bad timing in animation sticks out like a sore thumb.

You must remember that the audience will usually be seeing your film for the first time. As the animator, you need to guide them and tell them exactly where to look at each point in the film. The audience perceives things best sequentially, so you should present your main actions that way, one at a time, within a smooth sequence of motions. A character stubs his toe, recoils, and then reacts. If the reaction is too quick, the audience won't have time to "read" it; the recoil acts as a bridge between the two main actions.

A character **stubs his toe**. **He recoils,** so the audience can see the force against the toe. **The character then reacts.** The timing between these actions will determine how well the scene reads.

Think of a Road Runner cartoon. When Wile E. Coyote steps out over the gorge, he takes a while to notice that he's suspended in midair. He'll typically react, then look directly at the camera with a pitiful expression. This one drawing can be held for almost a second. He may blink or his whiskers may twitch, but it is essentially a still pose. He then will zip off the screen in a few frames. This is a great example, because in the span of time that the pose is held, the audience comes to the same realization as the coyote—he's doomed. It also draws the audience's full attention to the coyote, so that when he does fall off screen, they see that clearly as well.

One of the most important lessons you can learn about timing, then, is to draw attention to what is about to move before it moves. An action reads only when the audience is fully focused on it. As the animator, you must guide the audience's eyes through the character's actions.

Arcs and Natural Motion

Objects tend to move along arcs. This is because an object is usually subject to multiple forces, all simultaneously acting upon the object. The exceptions are usually mechanical motions, which tend to be more linear.

With characters, arcs are also created by the natural mechanics of the body. Joints in the body move by rotating, and this rotation creates arcs.

Natural objects move along arcs.

Mechanical motions are more linear.

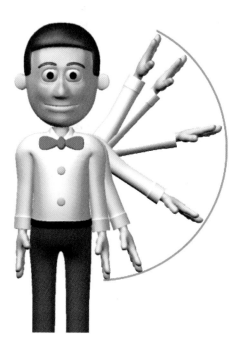

The motion of an arm is dictated by the rotation of the joints, which trace out arcs. If the end of the arm traced out a straight line, it would appear unnatural.

Other parts of the body also trace arcs. For example, a simple head turn traces an arc rather than a straight line.

Forward Kinematics, Inverse Kinematics, and Arcs

When joints are animated using forward kinematics, they move by rotating. These rotations automatically move a character's joints along arcs. Such motion is anatomically correct and has a natural look, and it can be produced with little effort.

Limbs animated using inverse kinematics, however, need a little more attention. While inverse kinematics is a very helpful tool for locking the legs or arms to a specific location, it works through translation rather than rotation. This means that the software will use translation to move the limb between the keyframes, creating a straight line and also an unnatural motion. To correct for this, you may have to add a few extra keyframes or tweak the motion curves to get a more natural arc.

Rotating the joints using forward kinematics naturally creates an arc.

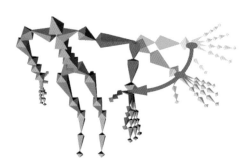

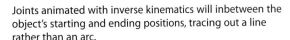

Joints animated with inverse kinematics will inbetween the object's starting and ending positions, tracing out a line rather than an arc.

Adding an extra keyframe or adjusting the motion graphs can turn the line into a more natural arc.

Force and Drag

When animating, we also need to consider the effects of drag on an object. A force transmitted to an object does not affect all parts of the object equally. Imagine two sticks connected by a flexible joint. If you pulled one of the sticks straight down, the second stick would take a while to "get in line." This effect is called drag.

Another point to consider is the way a multijointed object will move. If an object has more than two joints, each joint will drag behind the one before it. A third joint added to our stick simply drags behind the second.

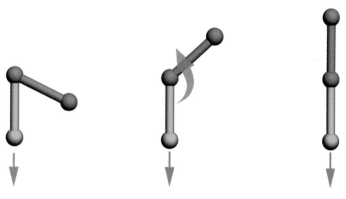

If you pull down on the first stick…

…the second stick must rotate to get into alignment with it.

Drag causes a delay before the two sticks line up.

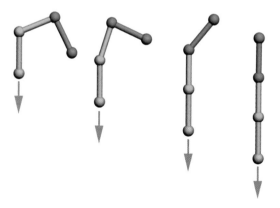

Three sticks simply means more drag. The third stick drags behind the second, which drags behind the first.

The same principles apply to the joints of your character. The spine is really just a collection of joints. Force transmitted to one end of the spine takes time to reach the other end. Force applied to the hand takes time to reach the shoulder and even longer to reach the feet. Think of a dog's tail. The joints in the tail behave exactly like the joints in our stick example. The base of the tail rotates in a arc, causing the outer parts of the tail to drag.

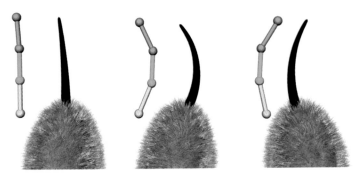

A dog's tail behaves exactly like our sticks: the end of the tail drags behind the base.

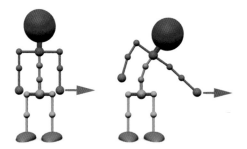

Much like the sticks, the body's skeleton is really just a collection of joints. Force applied to one joint of the skeleton takes time to reach the other joints.

Squash and Stretch

Most objects tend to flex and bend as they move. Think of a rubber ball. If you apply a force to the top of it, the ball will compress or "squash." If you pull the ball from both ends, it will stretch.

The fact that objects can change shape when subjected to forces is helpful when animating. You can give a ball bouncing on the ground a "rubbery" feel by squashing it as it hits the ground and stretching it as it takes off.

This principle applies to character animation as well. Characters subjected to forces will change shape just as a ball does, but in a more complex way. Think of a gymnast—when a character jumps in the air, she'll stretch as she takes off, and when she lands, she'll squash to absorb the force of landing.

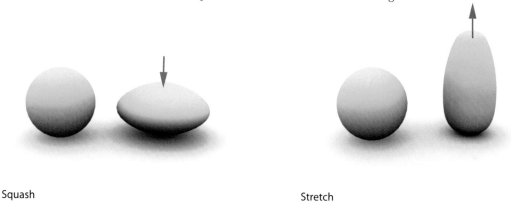

Squash   Stretch

Squash and stretch in a character

Squash and stretch are particularly important because people tend to perceive the outlines of objects first. When a character is squashed, the outline is compact. When the character stretches, the outline changes completely, giving the eye a lot of visual contrast.

In character animation, there are many levels of squash and stretch. In a naturalistic setting, a character may "squash" simply by bringing its limbs close to the body and "stretch" by extending the limbs. In a more cartoony environment, the squash and stretch may actually change the physical shape of the character, making it appear more rubbery.

When squashing and stretching, you must remember to maintain your character's volume. Consider a balloon filled with water. If you stretch it or squash it, the water in one part of the balloon simply moves to another

As the character "squashes," it appears more compact.

As it "stretches," the character elongates, much as the rubber ball did.

Extreme squash and stretch might not be totally realistic, but it can sure be fun to animate and watch.

area, but the volume doesn't change. The same principle applies to characters: No matter how squashed or distended the character, its volume should
always remain the same. If the volume increases or decreases, it will appear
as though the character is growing or shrinking.

This is not stretching; it is the character gaining weight.

If one part of the body expands, another must contract to maintain volume.

This flour sack is a good example of the way volume remains constant while shape can squash and stretch.

Anticipation

Anticipation is the body's natural way of gaining momentum before an action begins. When people jump, they swing their arms behind them, bend their knees, and actually move *down* slightly to get momentum before jumping up. In baseball, a batter will move the bat back before swinging it forward. You lean back before getting out of a chair. It's kind of like getting a head start on the action.

Before this character pitches the ball, he "winds up" and anticipates the throw.

Anticipation can also be used to direct the audience's attention. This character's hand goes up, signaling to the audience that something is going to happen. Once he has the audience's attention, he completes the action.

Anticipation is a natural part of motion, and by exaggerating it, we can keep the audience's attention and achieve crisper timing. The human eye is naturally drawn to things that move. Moving an object in the opposite direction of its eventual motion draws attention to the object before it makes the important move. When it does move, the audience is already watching, so the motion can be much faster without confusing viewers.

You'll often need to animate an action that takes place very quickly, such as a "zip out." When you do, your audience needs to be fully aware of the action before it occurs, making anticipation of the action very important.

Before leaping off the box, the flour sack anticipates the jump by bending over.

Overshoot

As we've seen, anticipation is used to make an action's beginning more life-like. At the tail end of the action, we have "overshoot." In many cases, a character's body will not come to a slow and perfect stop. Instead, it will overshoot the stopping point for a few frames and then settle into the pose. Like anticipation, it is a natural part of motion that can be exaggerated to the animator's advantage.

When a character throws out his arm to point his finger, his arm will anticipate the move before the action starts. If the motion is quick, the character's arm will naturally overshoot the pose so that the arm is absolutely straight. After a few frames, the arm will then settle into a more natural, relaxed pose. Overshoot can be used to give your character's actions more snap. If you're animating from pose to pose, you can overshoot a pose for a few frames and then settle in.

When this character throws out his arm, he overshoots the final pose and then settles in. This usually happens in just a few frames, but it gives the action more snap.

Secondary Action

When animating a character, you'll focus mainly on the primary motion of the body and the limbs. While this creates the broad motion, most characters have lots of other little details that need attention. Clothing, hair, jewelry, and even the fat on the belly need to move properly to truly bring the scene to life.

These little details fall into a broad category known as secondary action, which include the tweaks, gestures, and little touches that add extra life and personality to your character. It could be as simple as animating a dog's floppy ears, or it could be more subtle, such a baby in a high chair wiggling her toes while she eats. The primary action is eating, but the secondary action, wiggling the toes, adds personality and life to the character as a whole.

Secondary action is best animated as a layer on the primary action. First animate the main motion, and when this is correct, add the secondary actions. They should be little extra touches and not detract from the main point of the shot.

Remember, the cardinal rule in animation is to do one thing at a time. The secondary actions serve as a nice, subtle bridge between the main actions, but if they get too wild or noticeable, they will become primary actions themselves and detract from the shot.

This dog's collar bounces around on its neck as it walks. The collar is not the primary motion of walking, but its secondary action adds realism to the scene.

The flourish of this character's fingers can also be considered secondary action because they are minor motions compared to the primary motion of the body.

Follow-Through

When a character comes to a stop, not every part of his body will stop on the same frame. Momentum will carry some parts of the body past the stopping point. The parts of the body still moving are said to follow through. Think of a dog with big, floppy ears. The ears continue to follow through after the dog has stopped, behaving much like a pendulum.

In many ways, follow-through and overshoot are the same thing, because a part of the body goes past the stopping point and then settles back. The big difference is that follow-through is a secondary action that happens on almost any motion.

Overlap

Overlap is similar to follow-through in that it involves secondary action of the body. But unlike follow-through, which usually happens at the end of a motion, overlap usually happens during a motion or a cycle of motions.

As the body moves, parts of the body initiate the primary motion, but other parts of the body drag behind. A heavy person's belly, for example, will drag behind the motion of the legs. As the legs push the body up, the belly takes a while to get going and drags behind for a few frames. As the body moves down, the belly drags in the opposite direction. When the walk begins to cycle, the cycle of the belly overlaps it.

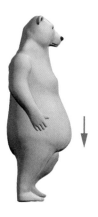

Follow-through allows some parts of the body, such as this dog's floppy ears, to move past the stopping point.

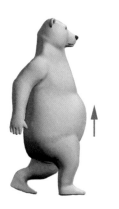

The motion of the belly on this character overlaps the motion of the walk cycle.

Automating Secondary Action

One of the nice things about computers is that they can do a lot of the mundane chores. In traditional animation, animating the secondary action of a character can be a job in itself. Having the computer calculate the secondary action automatically can save a ton of time. Still, as with any automated procedure, it must not be taken for granted. The animator should pay attention to these solutions and make corrections as needed.

Moving Holds

Your character may need to hold a pose or be still for anywhere from a few frames to a few seconds. This is known as a hold. In cel animation, a hold is typically done by simply holding a single drawing on the screen for the duration of the hold. In computer animation, this is the kiss of death. A digital character held in a single position for more than a few frames will completely die—it will look as though you hit the pause button.

Even something as simple as the secondary action of a character's antennae can be automated by adding a simple expression to the bones that deform it.

A character left immobile on the screen will look as though you hit the pause button.

Instead, move the character slightly over the duration of the hold. Here, the character has shifted his weight to his left slightly. Be sure to overlap these motions.

Basic Character Animation

In this tutorial, we will animate the character you built in the previous chapters to perform a simple jump. This jump will cover all the fundamental components of motion. I will give you approximate timing of the motions, but each character and situation is different, so use these numbers as a rough guide only. You'll need to adjust your timing until you like it. The basic rule is that if it looks right, then it is right.

Set up the scene by creating a simple plane for the floor, as well as a box. Place the character on top of the box. At frame 1, **create a more natural pose** for the charac-ter. Keyframe the major joints (arms, legs, spine, and head) to fix this pose.

We want the audience to read this pose, **so let's hold it for a short time**. Move the time slider ahead six frames and again set keyframes for the major parts of the body. Now we need to **anticipate the jump** by moving the character's arms back and bending the knees. Be sure to keep the character's weight balanced above the feet. Move forward six to eight frames and key this pose.

Again, the audience needs time to read the anticipation, so **move the slider forward four to six frames** and create a moving hold by extending this pose a little bit and keying it. **Now it's time for the leap.** Move the time slider forward four to six frames and key the extension of the body as the character leaps.

As the arms swing forward, they need to follow an arc. Scrub the animation or use a tool such as trajectories or ghosting to make sure the hands trace out a smooth curve. Now **we need to create two poses**, one at the top of the leap and the other where the character is "stretched" right before the landing. The arms should be back. The entire jump should take eight to twelve frames, so space your keyframes accordingly and make sure that the character's hips follow a parabola.

Move approximately two frames ahead and **create the pose of the character landing** and "squashing" as his body absorbs the shock of impact. The arms will drag behind the body a bit, so keep them back. This pose should happen fairly quickly after the previous pose to achieve maximum contrast.

Move the slider four to six frames ahead and **create an "overshoot" pose** where the character stands back up and gets ready to settle in. In this pose the head should be higher than in the next pose, where the character is standing normally. The arms will follow through and move upward, again along an arc. You may want to stretch the legs to their maximum extension and even have the character take a step at this point.

In another four to six frames, the character is "settling in" to another stable pose. Have the legs slightly bent, and place the weight over one foot.

Obviously, this is just a start of the animation, so go back over it and make sure the motions are smooth and natural. Adjust the timing if needed and make certain that all parts of the body follow arcs as they move through the scene.

Conclusion

As you've seen, motion can happen for a variety of reasons, but the basics of every motion are the same. All objects move because they are affected by forces, and all moving objects have momentum that makes it difficult to change their course. Additionally, the language of motion defines a number of other specific motions that help bring characters to life, such as anticipation, overshoot, and follow-through.

The best way to understand these concepts is to practice. Animate a lot of very simple scenes, using the fundamental motions described in this chapter.

CHAPTER FIVE

Creating Strong Poses

A pose is the way a character presents itself to the camera. If the character is sad, happy, frightened, or brave, you should be able to read that emotion in its pose. The way the character stands, where his hands are placed, and the position of the head all have a role in creating the pose. Like theater, dance, mime, and countless other performing arts, animation relies heavily on clear poses to convey a message.

Strong poses are one of the fundamental building blocks of animation. Even the simplest shots require that a character hit a strong pose: a pose that is ana-tomically correct, is pleasing to the eye, and conveys a message.

In addition to communicating your character's emotions, strong poses clarify action; the audience reads them well the instant they appear. As a result, the audience knows exactly what's happening and will understand your character's actions better.

Good poses also convey information about balance and weight.

Posing the Body Naturally

The first major component of any natural pose is balance. If a pose is out of balance, the character will appear as if it's about to tip over. For the purposes of posing, the body is a system of joints that is constantly trying to stay in balance. Each bone acts as a tiny lever that distributes the weight of the body through the spine to the hips, then down through the legs to the ground. A pose even slightly out of balance will be seen by the audience as "wrong."

The second main component of a natural pose is anatomical correctness. Each joint in the body has limited motion, and keeping the joints within their natural limits keeps the pose looking natural. If part of the body is out of place, the audience will pick up on it and the character will seem "wrong." Of course, there are exceptions to this rule, such as cartoon characters that stretch their joints beyond realistic limits.

Posing the Hips and Torso

In the human body, the hips support the weight of the upper body and distribute it through the legs to the ground. They're the place to start when creating a balanced pose. If a character picks up an object, for example, the object's weight will need to be balanced by the rest of the body—usually by adjusting the hips.

Poses need to remain balanced.

Joints need to remain within their natural limits if you're posing naturalistic characters.

The hips are the foundation of any pose your character takes. As we have seen, adjusting the hips changes the body's center of balance. Any change to the hips will throw the character off balance and initiate an action. In animation, most motions start with the hips because most motions begin with a change in the character's balance.

The hips are also part of the torso, which contains most of the mass of the body. Balance is about weight distribution, so balancing the massive torso goes a long way toward balancing the entire body. To balance the torso, you'll need to adjust the spine and shoulders in concert with the hips to keep everything in line. A simple example of this would be a standing pose. In a relaxed stance, the body usually rests on one leg, not both. If you've ever watched people waiting in a long line, you'll see that people constantly shift their weight from one foot to another as they wait. Rarely do they place their weight equally on both feet, except when standing at attention. This means that even when posing a character that is just standing there, you still need to pay attention to the character's balance.

Rarely does a person stand on both feet. Placing the weight on one foot creates a more natural pose.

This pose is unbalanced. The character's upper body puts his weight too far forward, which makes him unstable.

If you move the hips back, the weight of the character becomes centered over the feet, stabilizing the pose.

Lifting the additional weight affects the balance again. The hips must move even further back to balance the load.

When the hips are over one leg, the weight of the free leg pulls the hips out of center.

When a person rests on one leg, it throws the whole torso off center. The simplest way to think about this is that when the weight is on one leg, the free leg pulls the hip down and out of balance. To compensate, the body must curve the spine, which forces the shoulders in the opposite direction to maintain balance.

Almost every pose starts with hip placement; the second step is to counterbalance the hips using the spine and shoulders. Typically, this means rotating the shoulders in opposition to the hips, but there are many balanced poses that use other counterbalancing techniques.

Posing Legs and Feet

The legs and feet are the support system for the entire body. When a character stands, all of its weight is transmitted to the ground through the legs. The weight of the body causes the legs to bend slightly. When the weight is over one leg, the other leg can be a little bit straighter because it has less weight on it.

To maintain balance, the upper body must compensate by adjusting the spine so the weight remains centered over the weight-bearing leg.

When the body is about to move, the legs will bend; they will then straighten as they move the body from one pose to another. When a character comes to a stop, the legs also act as shock absorbers, bending at the knee to absorb energy.

While the legs and feet both support a character's weight, the feet are used more for balance. Most of a character's weight rests on the heel of the foot. This lets the ball of the foot and the toes act as levers to fine-tune the character's weight distribution. Rarely will a character's feet point straight ahead. Typically, the toes will point outward, though sometimes a character will be pigeon-toed.

Weight over the right leg causes the knee to bend.

The knees are another important part of the body to consider during posing. Knees bend and straighten, but the direction of the knee can also be critical to the pose. Knees almost always follow the angle of the foot.

Drop the hips when a character shifts its weight.

Rarely do the feet point straight ahead (left); the more natural pose has the toes pointed outward (right).

The knees naturally point in the same direction as the feet.

Posing Hands and Arms

Actors who take to the stage for the first time are always very self-conscious about what to do with their hands. Animators often have the same problem.

The hand is a complex structure and is one of the most difficult parts of the body to pose. The best way to pose the hand is to understand a little bit about how it works. Generally, the index finger is the dominant digit of the hand, with the other fingers decreasing in dominance, down to the pinky. This dominance can be seen in a relaxed pose because the outer fingers tend to curl up more, while the index finger remains straighter.

This hand is not in a natural pose and looks very stiff.

A more natural pose has the fingers relaxed. Notice how the pinky curls in before the index finger.

The index finger is the dominant finger.

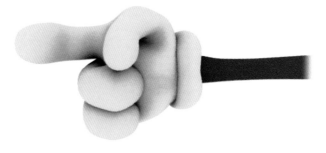

As the hand tightens into a fist, notice how the less dominant fingers curl first.

Grasping and Manipulating Objects

Hands can grasp, hold, and manipulate objects in a wide variety of ways. For a heavy object, the entire hand may be used, while delicate objects are manipulated with just the fingers. Achieving a good pose requires nothing more than looking at your own hands as they perform the same task.

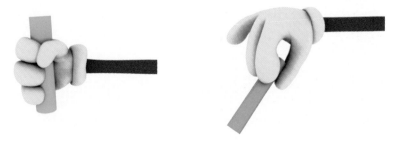

An object such as a handle can be grasped simply by curling all the fingers around it.

More delicate manipulation is possible by using the fingertips.

Holding a pencil is another way the hand can manipulate an object.

Creating Appealing Poses

In addition to being physically correct, your poses must also be presented so that they convey the character's intent to the audience in a clear and aesthetically pleasing way. Remember that your 3D animated creation is almost always going to be shown on a 2D screen. The screen is your stage, and one of the best ways to pose characters for the camera is to study and reproduce methods pioneered by magicians, mimes, and stage actors over the centuries. Good silhouettes and a strong line of action will help present your characters to the camera properly.

Symmetry can also show up in facial animation.

Avoiding Symmetry

Since the body is so symmetrical, it is very tempting to place it into symmetrical poses. Not only is this dull and boring, it's very unnatural. To keep your characters looking natural, you'll need to keep their poses and movement asymmetrical in almost every way—from the positions of the eyes, hands, and feet to their motions and actions. Symmetry has an odd habit of creeping in at the worst times.

Making a face less symmetrical adds interest.

Avoiding symmetry means watching out for what animators call "twins." A twin is a part of the body that mirrors another. Even minor details in a pose—such as both feet pointing in the same direction—can make a character look strange.

This pose is symmetrical in almost every respect. It is also boring in almost every respect.

This pose breaks symmetry in a number of places, and is more interesting for it.

Creating Strong Silhouettes

One of the fundamentals of good posing is presenting a strong silhouette to the audience or, in our case, the camera. Because the human eye is designed to notice contrast, it usually picks out an object's silhouette first and then fills in the rest of the detail. If an action is presented so that its outline is clear, the action will be clear as well.

Think of a magician pulling a rabbit out of a hat. He always pulls the rabbit out to either his right or his left. That way, even the person in the back row can understand what's going on. If the magician wants to hide something, he'll usually do it when his hands are passing in front of his body. The body, along with the motions, serves to conceal the action. The exact same principles apply to animation. Animators usually won't have to worry about performing sleight of hand, but they're very concerned about making actions readable. The silhouette is the key.

To check out your character's silhouette, simply pose your character in the computer. Next, apply a matte black texture to the character. Render the pose. You'll have nothing but the silhouette. Another way to go about it is to simply look at the alpha channel matte used to composite the character into the shot—it's always the silhouette.

Once you have this image, ask yourself, "What is this character doing?" If your silhouette is clear, the action and the pose will read well.

A good silhouette will tell you what this character is doing…

…he's about to pull something from his hat. If the silhouette reads well, so does the pose.

A good example of silhouetting is this kick. The image reads well both as an image and in silhouette.

Turn the camera 90 degrees, however, and nothing reads. The angle from which you view your character is as important as the pose itself.

Strong Line of Action

In addition to having a strong silhouette, a good pose should have a definite line of action. This is a strong line that you can follow from your character's feet to the tips of its fingers. This line not only makes your pose more effective, it also adds beauty to the pose. The human eye is naturally drawn to a good line.

For example, if your character is throwing a ball, arch the back and make the arm follow the same arc. This will give a much more pleasing line than if the arm just moves back. If you put the whole body into the throw, it will look more convincing.

This pose is weak because it has a weak line of action.

Getting the character's whole body into the action creates a stronger line of action as well as a stronger pose.

As the ball is tossed, the line of action reverses to add contrast to the pose.

The line of action affects every part of a character's body. If a character is in a tug-of-war, he'll dig his heels into the ground and arch his back, putting every muscle he can into the effort. Even simple actions should follow a definite line. If a character is proud, he'll arch his back and throw out his chest. If he's tired, he'll slump over and have a completely different arc. Even subtle details, such as the placement of a finger or toe, can have a profound effect on a pose.

This tug-of-war pose shows a great line of action.

If a character is tired, he'll slump over in a different line of action.

The **thumb breaks** the line of action in the arm. **Adjusting the thumb** creates a stronger line, as does pointing the toe.

Animating with Poses

In the golden age of animation, animators discovered that there were two basic methods for animating a scene: straight ahead and pose to pose. Each method uses posing differently and has its own place and its own advantages.

Pose-to-Pose Animation

Pose-to-pose animation is the more controlled of the two methods. In this method, you plan out your shot and then get the main poses of the character within the shot you've blocked out. If your character is standing up from a chair, for example, the poses might be leaning back, grabbing the armrest for support, leaning forward, and finally standing up. A character winning the lottery may read the lottery ticket and show disbelief, shock, and then joy.

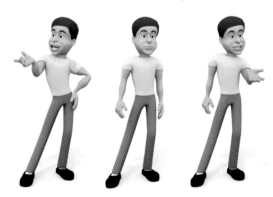

The theory is that every action can be broken down into a series of distinct poses. From there, it's a matter of creating inbetweens or letting the computer inbetween the poses for you and, of course, tweaking these as necessary. Pose-to-pose animation is used primarily for acting and dialogue, because each pose can be fit to the major points in the dialogue track. It is also used to animate difficult and tightly choreographed shots.

This character speaking dialogue was animated using the pose-to-pose method.

Strong poses also add clarity to actions such as this martial arts kick.

Straight-Ahead Animation

Straight-ahead animation is pretty much what the name implies. In this method, you start at frame 1 and animate "straight ahead" from there. It is used primarily in animation involving broad actions, such as walking, running, and other athletic activities.

Straight-ahead is more improvisational in nature and can sometimes lead to very spontaneous and complex motion. It's the method closest to "acting" a frame at a time, and is very similar to the techniques used in stop-motion animation. If you are trying to achieve a stop-motion look and feel, this is certainly the way to go. Keep in mind, though, that this method can make it hard to achieve well-defined and solid poses and thus sometimes produces animation that is hard to read. It also makes it difficult to animate complex shots.

Straight-ahead animation works well for athletic actions, such as this leap.

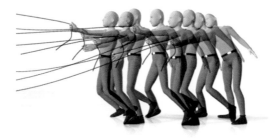

Intermittent motions, such as this character being pulled by a rope, can also be animated using the straight-ahead method for more spontaneity.

Combining the Two Methods

You can combine pose-to-pose and straight-ahead animation and get the best of both; computer animation gives you the bonus of being able to do this rather easily. Most fast machines can play back an animation test almost instantly. This makes it easy for you to block out a series of poses rather quickly, almost in a straight-ahead fashion, or to animate a frame at a time in those sections that might need more spontaneity.

The question that still remains, however, is one of thought process. How do you approach animating your scene—do you plan your shot carefully (pose-to-pose) or do you improvise (straight-ahead)? This is not an easy question to answer, and the best advice is to use your intuition and experience. Over-planning a shot may very well sap the life out of it. Improvisation can add unexpected touches and details you would never have dreamed of. On the other hand, complex shots need to be planned out very carefully or the elements won't sync up.

Managing Poses

Many times, you will simply create poses as you go, but for larger projects, it may make sense to work from a library of poses that you've set up in advance. Getting a pose right can be a time-consuming process, and once you have a pose nailed down, it makes a lot of sense to hang on to it. Many software packages have incorporated features that help the animator manage poses.

Timeline-Based Libraries

One of the simplest ways to manage poses is to build your library in the scene file itself. Many animators use the frames below zero on the timeline as a pose library. Each frame has a discrete pose, and these poses can be saved with the master version of the character, so that whenever the character is placed in a new scene, the poses follow along.

Animating with this type of library is very straightforward: you locate the pose in the library and copy the keys representing this pose to the desired spot on the timeline. You can copy all the keys in the character for the entire pose or copy smaller sets of keys to isolate specific body parts, such as an arm or a hand.

These poses are stored in the "negative" frames of the scene. You can copy a pose into the main scene simply by selecting the appropriate keys and dragging.

File-Based Libraries

Another way to build a library is to build the poses as individual files and store them on a disk or server. This method requires that you be able to store poses or animation separately from the character. Software packages such as Maya and Softimage XSI allow poses and animation to be applied to a character from a file.

Similarly, nonlinear animation systems—which allow you to create, edit, and mix animation much as a nonlinear video editing system does—can be a great way to do pose-to-pose animation. As in the previous method, the poses are stored in a separate library on a hard disk or server and can then be dragged into the nonlinear editor to create the animation.

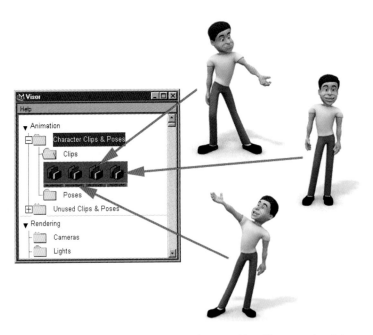

Some applications, such as Maya, allow poses to be stored in a library on the disk.

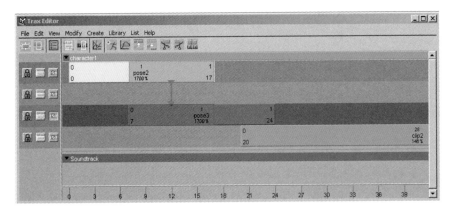

Packages with nonlinear animation editors allow you to animate with poses by dragging them into the editor.

Working with Poses

Regardless of how the poses are managed, the actual process of animating is essentially the same. Once you have the sequence of poses visualized in your head, you can simply copy the raw poses from the library to the proper spots on the timeline and then fine-tune the animation as needed.

One sticky issue that may arise is the huge number of animatable attributes that make up a character. A single character may contain dozens of joints, and managing all of those keys can be very confusing.

To help you manage this plethora of parameters, some packages, such as Maya, allow you to define a "character." This feature allows the grouping of all the keyable attributes of a character into an easily referenced collection, which permits keys to be set on the entire character at once. It also gives you more global control of the character because each pose can be represented by a single key, rather than many keys. This certainly makes it easier to block out poses as you animate, but you still have to go to individual curves to fine-tune individual parts of the character.

For more discrete control, many 3D applications allow you to create "subcharacters" so you can have separate keys for the arms and hands, for example. Software with predefined skeletons, such as Autodesk's Biped and Maya's Motionbuilder, build this feature into the skeletons.

Creating Pose-to-Pose Animation

In its simplest sense, pose-to-pose animation is just a series of poses that happen over time. This means that pose-to-pose animation has two important elements: poses and time. To create successful pose-to-pose animation, you need to have terrific poses that are presented with the proper timing. Up to this point, we have talked a lot about what a makes a good pose. Now let's talk about how to turn those poses into animation.

Visualizing Your Scene

When animating using the pose-to-pose method, it's always best to visualize the scene first by acting it out in your head and thumbnailing the rough poses on paper. If you're animating to dialogue, you need to listen to the sound track and understand the major poses you want your character to hit. For action without dialogue, you need to understand the nature of the action and create the appropriate poses.

When creating the poses, be sure each pose clearly conveys the character's mood. You also need to pay attention to how poses flow together. It's best to have good contrast between adjacent poses so that each pose reads better. The lines of action in a character are a good indicator of contrast. Lines of action should follow a "whip" action, alternating their directions of curvature.

Once you have the basic poses mapped out, you need to create those poses within the scene. If you're working from a library of poses, simply drag the poses from the library to the proper place on the timeline. If you're creating the poses from scratch, you'll need to pose the character at the proper points in the scene.

Thumbnailing poses on paper can help you understand a scene.

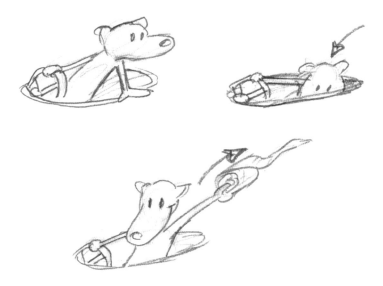

Regardless of how the poses are created, the end result will be a series of poses on the timeline. This is a good starting point, but if you play back the animation, you'll see the character move quickly from one pose to the next, with no definition. This sort of continuous motion is fine for flowing movements, such as running or a leap. Generally, however, you'll want your character to hold each pose so the audience can read it better.

Poses should clearly convey the character's mood.

Vary the line of action within a character to get good contrast between poses.

Creating Holds

A hold simply keeps a pose on the screen for a specified period of time. Poses can be held for anything from a few frames to several seconds. Creating holds in your animation will give the audience time to read and process the information you are giving them. It also gives your characters time to process information. A hold is a very important tool for timing. Comedians will often use pauses and holds to perfect the timing of a joke, for example, and the same goes for animation.

Take a simple example. A character lifts up a gift box, looks inside, and is pleasantly surprised. Here we have three poses, but the timing of the poses can affect how the audience perceives the character.

The easiest way to create a hold is simply to copy the pose down the timeline. This will duplicate the pose and give the pose a start and an end time, with the result being a hold. If you do this for each pose that requires a hold, you'll have the basic building blocks of a scene.

Three poses: the timing of each one affects the way the animation plays.

Duplicating a pose creates a hold.

You can rough out the timing of the scene by adjusting the start times of the poses and by moving the end times to increase or decrease the length of the holds. By adjusting the timing of these keys, you can completely fine-tune the timing of your scene.

When creating holds, you don't want the character to completely "freeze," so alter the second pose or create an inbetween pose. When a character is held in a pose, there are still forces acting upon it. Gravity, for example, will tend to pull a character downward. This may be expressed within the pose in a number of ways. A character's outstretched limbs may drift downward, or the hips may lower slightly, but the general rule of thumb is that the character tends to drift down during a hold.

A moving hold will keep the character alive. The weight of this character's nose will cause it to drift downward.

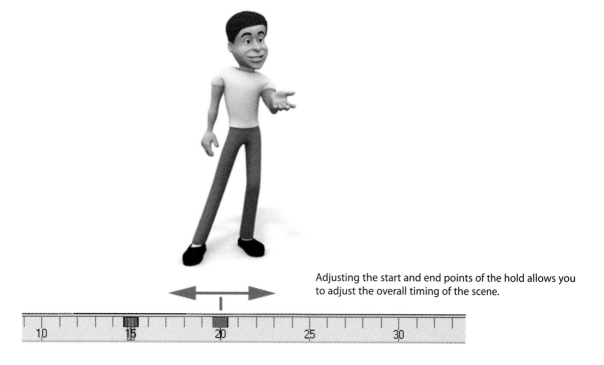

Adjusting the start and end points of the hold allows you to adjust the overall timing of the scene.

Transitioning Between Poses

Pose-to-pose animation is not as simple as dragging a few poses to the time-line and letting the computer do the inbetweens. Once you have the basic timing blocked out, you will still need to add all of the other little motions that make each pose flow into the next. Doing this involves attention to detail and knowledge of the basic principles of animation outlined in the previous chapter; you'll want to use anticipation, follow-through, arcs, and all the other principles we've discussed.

When a character begins a transition to another pose, you should anticipate that transition. Typically, this means dropping the hips so the character can shift its weight, but other parts of the body may also join in the anticipation. The hand may move inward before going into an outstretched pose, for example.

Anticipate the transition between poses.

During the transition, pay attention to arcs.

As the character reaches the new pose, be sure to over-shoot the pose, and then settle into the actual pose.

During the transition, make sure that the major parts of the body move along arcs. This is particularly noticeable in the extremities, especially the hands and feet, but it applies to all parts of a character.

As you complete the transition, the character will tend to overshoot the final pose and settle in. To do this, simply push the pose past its intended position and let the computer do an inbetween to settle it into the final pose.

Breakdown Poses

If you let the computer inbetween a set of poses, the result will be a fairly smooth transition between them. In some cases, this will work perfectly well, but there are times when you'll want to help guide the inbetween. This can be accomplished using a breakdown pose, which is simply a third pose that lies between two extremes.

A simple inbetween. The hand hits the table.

The breakdown pose guides the inbetween, in this case making the hand hit the table more forcefully.

Breakdown poses can be used in a wide variety of ways. One example might be a simple head movement. A character may want to lead the motion with his chin. Movement of a hand may change the angle of the wrist during the motion to get more snap. In fact, just about any set of extremes can have a breakdown pose added to give more character to the inbetween.

A character gestures with a simple in between.

Adding a breakdown pose in the middle adds a flourish to the motion.

Pose-to-Pose Animation

Let's create some very simple scenes using pose-to-pose animation. These will allow you to explore the areas of posing and timing.

For the first exercise, we will do a bit of personality animation. Create a box in the same scene as your character. Have your character do three things:

1. Notice the box.
2. Look inside the box.
3. React to what's inside the box.

Each one of these three actions will require a pose, but you will probably need additional poses to flesh out the scene.

The second exercise is more athletic and will explore the smooth transition between poses. Create a ball in the same scene as your character. Have the character pick up the ball, look at it, then rear back and throw it. When the character throws the ball, be sure to have it anticipate the throw, as well as overshoot the final pose. Pay attention to arcs, particularly during the throw.

Let's take a look in the box, shall we?

Pick up the ball and toss it.

Conclusion

This chapter has focused on the importance of posing and staging your characters. Remember to keep your poses natural and balanced. Avoid symmetry in your poses, and also be sure to keep a strong line of action and silhouette. You must always keep in mind that your audience sees your animation only through the camera. The best animation you can create won't come across if the camera doesn't see it properly.

CHAPTER SIX

Walking and Locomotion

Animating a pose at a time is good for some types of animation, but many times your character will need to move from place to place. This means animating the character walking, running, or using some other form of locomotion. Locomotion requires an intimate knowledge of balance and weight distribution, and learning to animate a walk is a skill every animator must master.

On top of the simple mechanics of walking, a character's walk conveys a great deal about its personality and mood. Every individual has a unique walk, and understanding how to personalize a walk will go a long way toward making a character come alive.

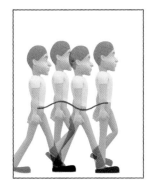 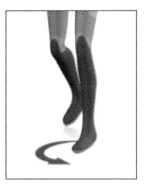  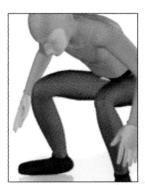

The Mechanics of Walking

Before you actually animate a walk, you'll need to understand the mechanics of walking. Walking is a good exercise in balance and control.

Walking has been described as "controlled falling." Every time you take a step, you actually lean forward and fall slightly, throwing your body out of balance. When you catch your weight with your outstretched foot, the body moves back into balance; if you failed to put your foot forward, you would fall flat on your face. After your foot touches the ground, your body's weight is transferred to it and your knee bends to absorb the shock. The front leg then lifts the body and propels it forward as the rear leg swings up to catch you again, and the cycle repeats.

Before you read any further, get up and walk around the room for a bit. Pay attention to how each part of your body moves. You'll soon notice that every part of the body, from the feet to the arms to the head, has its own unique set of motions. As you walk around, notice how you lean forward into the walk, and how your legs neatly catch your body to prevent it from falling. If you purposely hold your foot back on a step, you'll fall flat on your face.

The walk usually starts with the feet at the "extended position," where the feet are farthest apart and where the character's weight shifts to the forward foot.

As the weight of the body is transferred to the forward foot, the forward knee bends to absorb the shock. This position is called the "recoil position" and is the lowest point in the walk.

This figure illustrates the point halfway through the first step. As the character moves forward, the forward knee straightens out and lifts the body to its highest point. This position is called the "passing position" because the free foot passes the supporting leg at this point.

The process of walking is very complex: Not only do the feet have to move across the ground, but the hips, spine, arms, shoulders, and head all move in sync to keep the system in balance. Although these movements are complex, if you break them down joint by joint, the mechanics of walking become clear.

The following sections break down a basic walk, step by step. For clarity, I've animated a simple skeleton so you can see how each joint moves.

The Feet and Legs

The feet and legs propel the body forward by pushing the body out of balance, then catching the weight. Most walks are animated starting at the feet. To keep your character looking natural, you should always keep the joints bent slightly, even at full leg extension.

As the character moves forward, the weight-bearing foot lifts off the ground at the heel, transmitting the force to the ball of the foot. The body starts to fall forward. The free foot swings forward like a pendulum to meet the ground and catch the body's weight.

The free leg makes contact with the ground, completing half the cycle. The second half is an exact mirror of the first. If it differs, the character may appear to limp.

The Hips, Spine, and Shoulders

The body's center of gravity is at the hips; all balance starts there, as does the rest of the body's motion. During a walk, it's best to think of the hips' motion as two separate, overlapping rotations. First, the hips rotate along the axis of the spine, forward and back with the legs. If the right leg is forward, the right hip is rotated forward. Second, at the passing position, the free leg pulls the hip out of center, forcing the hips to rock from side to side. These two motions are then transmitted through the spine to the shoulders, which mirror the hips to maintain balance.

When the feet are fully extended, the hips must rotate along the axis of the spine. To keep balance, the shoulders swing in the opposite direction. From the front, the spine is relatively straight, but from the top, you can see how the hips and shoulders twist in opposite directions to maintain balance.

At the passing position, the front view shows the hip being pulled out of center by the weight of the free leg, causing a counter-rotation in the shoulders. From the top, the hips and shoulders are at nearly equal angles.

At the extension of the second leg, the hips and shoulders again are flat when viewed from the front. From the top, you can see the completed rotation of the hips and shoulders.

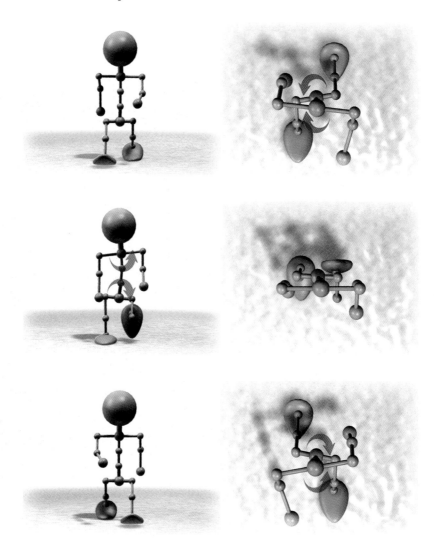

The Arms

Unless the character is holding something or gesturing, its arms generally hang loose at the sides. When walking, they act like pendulums, dragging a few frames behind the motion of the hips and shoulders. Even at full extension the arms should be slightly bent at the elbows, to keep them looking natural.

The Head and Spine from the Side

If you look at a character's spine from the side, you can see its general posture, which may be very stiff or slouched over, depending on the character's attitude. The spine also absorbs some of the shock transmitted to the hips from the legs, making it flex from front to back a bit.

The arms act like pendulums as they swing.

In a standard walk, the head tries to stay level, with the eyes pointing in the direction of the walk, but it bobs around slightly to stay balanced. If a character is excited, this bobbing is more pronounced. The head may also hang low for a sad character, or may look around if the scene requires it.

Because walking is kind of like falling forward, the body should be angled forward slightly at the hips for most walks. The spine arches up slightly to keep the chest and head over the hips. However, this line of action can change with the character's attitude.

For example, if a character is terribly sad, he tends to hunch forward and hang his head low. This posture forces the hips to rotate in the opposite direction, giving the body a different attitude. He'll most likely drag his feet as well.

Animating Walks

Now that you understand the underlying mechanics of walking, you can attempt to animate a walk. You'll need to understand how the walk is timed as well as the length of your character's stride. The mood and demeanor of the character will affect the style of the walk as well.

Timing the Walk

The first thing you need to concern yourself with is the timing of the walk. How many frames does a step take? That's not an easy question to answer, because you'll have to make a series of other decisions about your character. Is your character large and lumbering, or small and scrappy? Is your character running or walking? Happy or sad? All these factors determine the amount of time it takes your character to take a step.

At a normal walking gait, a step takes anywhere from one-third to two-thirds of a second, (8 to 16 frames at 24 fps, or 10 to 20 frames at 30 fps), with a half second per step being about average. A full cycle (both right and left steps) takes about a second per cycle. Larger characters tend to walk slower, and smaller characters walk faster. In general, men have slightly slower gaits than women, and sad people walk more slowly than happy people.

One nice thing about working with a computer is that many programs enable you to scale the length of your animation. If your character is walking too slowly, you can speed him up a bit by reworking the keys.

Stride Length

In a basic walk, the length of the legs and the speed of the walk will determine your character's stride. Generally, the faster a character walks, the longer the step. When animating a walk, the first pose you'll want to create is the extended position, where the legs transfer the weight from one leg to another.

Animating the Lower Body

The best way to create a walk is by working from the extreme poses and filling in the middle. You should create the two extended poses first, and then create the passing pose in the middle of these. Additional poses are created in between the extended and passing positions.

 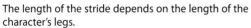 

The length of the stride depends on the length of the character's legs.

A character can take shorter steps if the mood calls for it.

When animating a walk, the first pose created is usually the extended position.

This extended pose is then mirrored with the opposite foot forward.

In the middle of these two poses, we create the passing position in which the free foot passes the supporting leg.

Halfway between the first extended position and passing position, we create a recoil, where the forward leg absorbs the weight of the body.

Looking at the way the body moves, we notice that the hips follow an up and down motion.

Animating the Upper Body

Once you've animated the basic leg movements, the next step is to create the upper body poses. The arms and shoulders mirror the motion of the hips and legs. When the right leg is forward, the right arm is back. The best way to create these poses is to use the same process as the legs—start with the extended positions and then do a middle pose. The arm motion drags behind the motion of the legs by a few frames, and always follows an arc.

Walk Cycles

Because walking is a cyclical motion, it may behoove you to create the walking motion as a cycle rather than as straight-ahead animation. If done properly, a cycle can save a great deal of time. One cycle can be applied to a number of different environments. Your character and his cycle can be placed just as easily in a cityscape as on a country road, because the walk motion is essentially the same. Why duplicate your efforts? Classical animators use this trick a lot, simply repeating the same sequence of drawings and swapping only the background painting, placing the character in a different location. In 3D, you have the flexibility to change the cameras, lighting, and environment to make the shot look completely different.

Those who work in the interactive and gaming industries deal with cycles every day. Most game engines require that you animate your characters in cycles, which are then called up as the player uses the game controls. In these cases, you may also need little animations to bridge the gap between cycles—between a walk and a run, for example.

When the right leg is forward, the right arm is back.

As the arm sweeps forward, it follows an arc.

As the arm moves back, it will tend to bend at the elbow.

There are two downsides to using cycles. First, because the cycle is repetitive, it can seem sterile and flat, particularly when viewed for an extended period of time. Second, cycles work best on level terrain. If your character has to walk around a corner or over a hill, the cycle might not match up properly.

Animating a cycle is similar to making your character walk on a treadmill. The body does not move forward; the feet simply move beneath it. To maintain the illusion of walking, the entire character must be moved across the ground (or the ground moved past the character) at the exact same rate that the feet are moving. Otherwise, the character's feet appear to slip. Also, the foot on the ground needs to move the exact same distance on each frame. Again, if the length of the steps varies, the feet appear to slip.

Animating Multiple Characters

When you're animating multiple characters, it's always tempting to make them walk at the same rate to simplify the animation process—but it's not a good idea. Giving your characters the same gait makes them look as though they're marching in unison, which can detract from the shot. It's always best to stagger walk cycles and to give characters different gaits. If one character is walking at 12 frames per step, give the other a gait that's slightly slower or faster, maybe 10 frames per step or 15. By mixing it up, you make your shots more varied and interesting.

This "multiple exposure" of a walk cycle shows that the body does not move forward; instead, the feet move beneath it. The red marks show how the foot on the ground moves the exact same distance on each frame to prevent the appearance of slipping.

Beyond Walking

Many animators think the walk is one of the key parts of a character's personality. John Wayne's walk is completely different than Groucho Marx's, for example. Knowing your character means knowing your character's walk. However, there are plenty of other ways to get around. Characters may also run, skip, sneak, shuffle, and tiptoe, among many others.

With that in mind, let's analyze a few other types of locomotion.

The Run

A run is more than just a fast and highly exaggerated walk. Instead of continuous falling, it's best to view a run as continuous leaping, with the body tending to lean forward a lot more. In a walk, one foot is always on the ground; in a run, there are times when both feet are airborne. The stride length also increases, making this distance longer than the feet could normally reach in a walk.

The timing of a run is faster than that of a walk, and can get down to a few frames per step. If you're animating an extremely fast run, motion blur is absolutely required to keep the feet and legs from strobing. Take a look at a running character and note the differences between a walk and a run.

This figure illustrates the "contact position." Notice that the body leans forward and the legs are farther apart than they are during a walk.

After contact is made, the forward leg absorbs the shock of the body at the "recoil position." As is the case in walking, this point is the lowest position in the cycle. Because the body is moving faster, momentum is increased, causing the bent leg to be even more exaggerated.

This figure illustrates a position similar to the "passing position" because it is halfway through the step. At this point in the cycle, the grounded foot pushes the body upward.

The body is now airborne and is at the highest point in the cycle.

The body lands and the next step starts. As in the walk, the second half of the cycle should be a mirror of the first.

The Skip

Another gait that is completely different from walking is the skip. In a skip, the character takes off and lands on the same leg, then switches legs for the next step. Even though the foot pattern is changed, the concepts of weight and balance do not. The character's hips, shoulders, and spine will all move in concert to keep the skeleton in balance.

This **skip**, animated by Angie Jones, shows the basic foot and body movements. The skip starts much like the walk, with the feet apart. A skip happens primarily on the toes, however.

As in the walk, the weight is transferred to the forward foot (or in this case, the forward toe).

The foot pushes off, sending the character into a small leap or hop. The opposite foot moves forward as the hips rotate.

  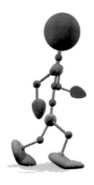

In the middle of the leap, the back leg moves forward slightly. The forward leg remains high and tucks under the body.

The character lands, but on the *rear* foot, with the forward foot staying high.

The forward foot touches down and the cycle repeats as a mirror of the first step.

The Sneak

Another favorite walk is the standard sneak. If you analyze it, this is just a variation of the basic walk, but the character is walking on his toes. It is a good example of how the basic walk can be modified to show character and mood. The main goal of a sneak is to walk quietly.

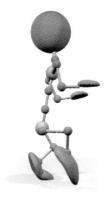

This **sneak**, animated by Angie Jones, starts much like the standard walk, but with the character on his toes. This makes the character slightly off center, so he extends his arms to regain balance.

The recoil position. Notice how the feet stay very close to the ground to help maintain balance.

The passing position. In the sneak, the planted leg does not extend nearly as much as in the walk.

Before the passing leg touches down, the character leans over at the waist to help maintain balance.

The cycle is finished and ready for the next leg.

Adding Personality to a Walk

Now that we understand the basic mechanics of walking, we can start adding some personality to the walk. How a character walks will tell you a lot about the character. An old person walks differently than a construction worker, who in turn walks differently than a fashion model. By shaping the character of the walk, you can give the audience a lot of information about your character.

Working with the Legs

The legs and feet are the foundation of the walk. Varying the way a character steps will affect how the walk appears to the audience. The width and length of the stride are two factors that can affect the character of a walk.

Stride Width

Varying the width of the stride can affect the perceived weight of the character. A wider stance is much more stable and indicates a heavier or stronger character. Placing the feet closer together makes the walk more delicate and feminine.

Animating the legs far apart creates a more stable walk.

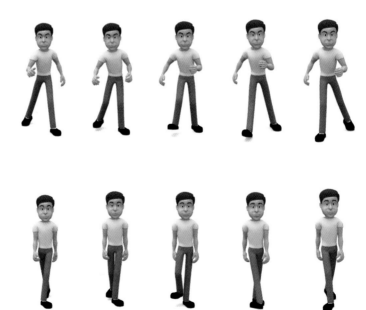

Animating the legs close together creates a more delicate walk.

Stride Length

A character's stride length can also affect the character of the walk. If a character is determined, purposeful, or in a hurry, he will generally take longer steps. A timid, sad, or wandering character will take shorter steps.

Generally, characters take steps of equal length. If one leg takes shorter steps, it will appear to limp. In a similar vein, placing one foot wide can add interest to a walk as well.

This character is in a hurry, so he walks with a long stride.

This sad character walks with a shorter stride.

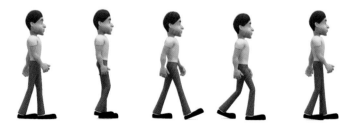

Using different strides on each leg creates a limp.

Working with the Hips

As a character walks, the hips will tend to sway from side to side. Amplifying or muting this motion can change the way the audience sees the walk. This motion is related to the stride width, as characters who walk with their feet closer together will need to sway the hips in order for the legs to pass each other. Women typically have more hip sway, the best example being runway models, who exaggerate this motion.

Working with the Arms

The way a character swings its arms can be very indicative of its mood and personality. While the typical arm motion of a walking character is to let the arms relax and swing like pendulums, adding a bit more purpose to this motion can add character.

A female character will typically walk with more hip sway.

As the feet move closer together, the sway becomes more pronounced.

A timid character may have very little arm movement…

…while a proud character's arm movement adds to his strut.

Transitions

Walking or running at a constant rate in a perfectly straight line makes for boring animation. Most characters start and stop, turn, and walk over varied terrain. Let's analyze some motion to look at ways to change such things as the speed and direction your characters travel.

Walk to Run

Since a run is a series of leaps, the transition from a walk to a run requires that the character leap. This particular transition occurs over one step, but characters may also speed up their walk and make the transition to a run over the course of several strides.

Start with a standard walk.

As the character begins to run, the body will lean forward.

A few frames later, the forward knee bends more as the character gets ready to leap. The shoulders rotate and the forward arm crosses in front of the chest.

The first step of the run. The body straightens out as the run begins.

Run to Walk

In the transition from a run to a walk, a character will need to absorb the energy of the run. Typically, this cannot happen in a single step, so the character takes progressively shorter steps over a span of several strides.

Start with a basic run.

As the character takes the last step of the run, the shoulders move back and the hips pivot forward. This allows the character to direct more energy into the leg and foot.

As the character lands, this energy is transferred through the leg as the knee bends to absorb the shock. The arms move outward from the body to maintain balance.

As the energy is dissipated, the character slows down to a walk.

Turns

Most walks and runs done as animation exercises are in a straight line. This looks great until your character needs to turn a corner. Turning a character is not a difficult task, but it does require a bit of extra attention.

A gentle turn, usually taking place over more than four or five steps, can be accomplished simply by turning the feet and hips slightly on each successive step. One thing to watch is the direction of the knees. Depending on how the character is set up, it may be very easy to turn the feet without affecting the knees. Be sure to rotate the legs at the thigh to maintain the proper knee direction. If your setup has null objects to control the knees, you can use those as well.

As the body turns, the shoulders will lean slightly toward the center of the turn. In a gentle turn, this will hardly be noticeable, but in a running turn, it might be more of a factor.

Single-Step Turn

If the character needs to turn quickly—say, in a step or two—you will probably need to pivot the feet. This is a fairly easy animation task, but make sure that the foot pivots at the ball of the toe and that this point of the foot doesn't slip.

Start with a basic walk. **As it begins to turn,** the character will start to pivot on the inside toe. The head will also begin to turn. **The shoulders counter-rotate** to maintain balance as the outside foot swings around. **The outside foot** sets down and the shoulders start rotating back. **The character takes one more step** and the walk continues as normal.

Running Turn

A run carries a lot more energy than a walk, so changing direction requires more effort. Just as a transition from a run to a walk may occur over several steps, a running turn may also take several steps, as the character needs to slow down before taking off in a different direction. Think of the way the silent movie comedians exaggerated running turns by hopping on one foot for several steps during the turn, almost like a car skidding to a stop.

Going Up and Down Slopes

Another consideration when creating walks and runs is where the character is traveling. If the character is on a slope, the incline will affect the posture of the character and how it walks or runs. This is because the character needs to remain relatively vertical against a sloping surface.

On a sloped surface, the character will still need to remain relatively vertical.

Start with a run. In a typical run, the upper body leans forward and the arms pump.

The character needs to slow before the turn. To do this, the arms stop pumping and the body leans back. This allows the forward foot to absorb more energy and reduce speed.

The body pivots on the right foot as the left foot swings forward and to the side.

The weight transfers to the left foot, and the body has the maximum lean into the turn. At this point, the left arm swings back by a large amount to gain energy.

The left leg bends to absorb the shock as the left arm swings around and the upper body twists.

As the left leg pushes off, the right leg takes a step to complete the turn and the upper body leans forward once again.

Walking Uphill

Since the character is essentially climbing against the force of gravity, a character walking uphill will expend more energy than one walking on a flat surface. To do this, the character will lean forward, and swing the arms more to get a bit more momentum as it goes up the hill. The character will also exert more effort as the leg lifts the body off of the ground, affecting the timing of the walk.

Walking Downhill

In a downhill situation, the character has gravity on his side. The force of gravity will tend to pull the character forward. On an extreme slope, the character may simply slide down the hill. On a typical slope, the character will lean back slightly and keep the arms out to maintain balance. The knees will also bend more as each foot sets down because the legs are acting as shock absorbers to dissipate the additional energy provided by gravity.

Jumping

A jump is a good example of how the body can store and release maximum energy by bending and moving joints to their extremes. This particular jump happens with both feet and is somewhat symmetrical.

When walking uphill, the character will lean forward and pump the arms more to get a bit more momentum as it goes up the hill.

When walking downhill, the character will lean back slightly and keep the arms out to maintain balance.

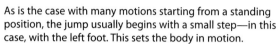

As is the case with many motions starting from a standing position, the jump usually begins with a small step—in this case, with the left foot. This sets the body in motion.

The left knee bends slightly as the right leg swings forward. The arms begin anticipating the jump by moving out and back slightly.

Before the big jump, the character takes a small hop to gain momentum. The left foot pushes off as both feet leave the ground. As this happens, the arms continue their anticipation by moving upward to the full extreme, gaining maximum energy.

Both feet land and plant firmly on the ground after the initial hop as the knees bend quite a bit to absorb the shock but also gain maximum energy. The arms are already rotating forward at the shoulders, with the elbows extended to get the maximum pendulum effect to begin the actual leap.

The legs straighten out and push the body upward. Adding to this is the momentum of the arms, which continue rotating forward and pull the body upward.

As the body reaches the apex of the jump, the character pulls the legs up toward the chest. This is to gain maximum momentum from the legs. The arms rotate forward as the torso leans forward. *(Continues on next page.)*

 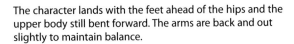

The character lands with the feet ahead of the hips and the upper body still bent forward. The arms are back and out slightly to maintain balance.

The momentum of the body bends the knees to absorb the shock. The upper body bends as an additional shock absorber as the shoulders almost touch the knees. The arms swing forward like a pendulum.

The character stands.

Leaping

Though many people use the words "leap" and "jump" interchangeably, a leap has one foot forward at the beginning the jump. It is like an extended step in a run, and is usually the type of jump performed while running.

The character starts on a run. The leap will start with the left foot.

As the character plants the left foot, the arms swing back.

As the left knee bends, the right leg and the arms swing forward and up, carrying the character's momentum upward.

The left leg pushes off as the character leaves the ground.

The right leg remains forward as the hips rotate forward, and the arms move outward to maintain balance.

The character lands on the right leg as the arms swing forward. At this point, the character can slow to a stop or keep running.

[**TUTORIAL**] ## Animating a Walk

This is a basic walk animated using inverse kinematics. While your particular rig may be a little different than the one in the exercise, the basic principles still apply.

When animating a walk, the first thing to decide is the timing. This walk is timed at 16 frames per step, 32 for one full cycle.

Start with a neutral skeleton.

Begin with the lower body. Create the first pose on the first frame. Position the left ankle forward, the right ankle back. Position the hips halfway between the feet. Rotate the hips along the vertical axis so that the left hip is slightly forward. Set position and rotation keys for all of these objects.

Move the slider to frame 8 to get the passing pose. Move the hips forward so that they are directly over the left ankle. Move the hips up so that the left leg extends to nearly straight. Rotate the hips along the vertical axis back to zero. Set position and rotation keys for the hip.

Now position the right leg. Move the right ankle so that it is directly above the left ankle and slightly below the left knee. Set a position key for the right ankle.

Create a pose that is the mirror of the first. Place the right ankle forward so that the foot rests firmly on the ground. Move the hips forward and down so that they are halfway between the feet. Rotate the hips along the vertical axis so that the right hip is slightly forward. Set position and rotation keys for all of these objects. Also set a position key for the left foot. Scrubbing the animation should show a rudimentary step.

We now need to tweak the step. Go back to the recoil position, where the hips sink as the weight is transferred to the forward foot. Move the hips down at this point and set a position key.

At the recoil position, the left foot needs to be rotated slightly downward. Rotate the foot and set a rotation key.

From a front view, go to frame 8, the middle of the cycle. At this point, the hips should be rotated slightly to the right due to the weight of the free right leg. Rotate the hips and set a rotation key. Scrubbing the animation should now show a basic lower body step.

Now move on to the upper body, starting with the spine. At frame 1, rotate the joints of the spine so that the shoulders mirror the hips. Set rotation keys for the spine.

Move to frame 8, the middle of the first step. Rotate the spine so the shoulders are even with the hips when viewed from above. From the front, rotate the spine so that the shoulders mirror the hips. Set rotation keys for the spine.

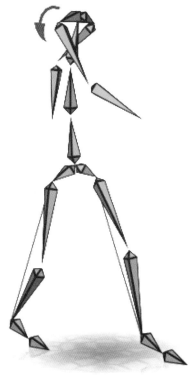

Move to frame 16. Adjust the spine so that it mirrors the pose on frame 1. Set rotation keys for the spine. The step is almost complete.

Now move on to the arms. With the right leg forward, the right arm needs to be back. Conversely, the left arm needs to be forward. Set rotation keys for these objects. Move to frame 16 and mirror these poses, setting rotation keys once again.

Now repeat the above sequence to create the left step. Once this is done, render a test.

In actual production, rather than working a step at a time, you would probably want to block out all of the steps first. Next, you would move on to the upper body and set all of the keys for a full cycle, then copy these keys for the duration of the walk.

Conclusion

As you have seen, animating a walk or a run requires a strong knowledge of weight and balance. Once you've mastered the basics of a walk, you can begin to add character to the walk by playing with the timing and spacing of your character's motions. Mastering these skills takes time and practice, so be sure to animate a lot of different characters walking and running in many different ways.

CHAPTER SEVEN

Facial and Dialogue Animation

Animating the face is one of the most challenging and rewarding tasks you will encounter as an animator. It requires a good knowledge of facial anatomy as well as a strong understanding of how mood affects facial expression. Facial animation is also intimately involved with animating dialogue.

Dialogue animation is always depicted as one of the more difficult skills to master, but while it is difficult, having a voice for your character can also be very helpful to the animation process. Try communicating the same information contained within a line of dialogue with body postures alone—it's like trying to ask for the restroom in a country where you don't know the language.

Dialogue communicates volumes of information to the audience. It also gives the animator a lot to use when creating a scene. The dialogue has an emotional content and tone of voice as well as a distinct rhythm that the animator can use for timing. After analyzing the dialogue track, the animator should know exactly which parts of the dialogue to emphasize during the scene. Dialogue animation also requires a good eye and a thorough knowledge of acting and emotion.

Animating the Face

Over the years, many methods have been used to animate the face. Early on in computer graphics, people tugged and pulled the vertices of the face—frame by agonizing frame—to make it move. Later on, people deformed the face directly through the use of bones, clusters, and lattices. All of these methods have their place, but they all have a number of weaknesses, the most important of which is a lack of control over the subtle details of the shape of the face.

Over time, most people learned that the best way to control these subtle details is in a modeling program. The only method that takes advantage of a modeling program is called morphing. In most productions, morphing has become the de facto standard method for animating faces. We covered the basics of modeling morph targets for animation in Chapter 3 and a face rigged with these targets is a great place to start.

Those who are learning facial animation should not start with dialogue animation, but with the simple act of conveying emotion. You don't need to have a character speak for it to be expressive. There are plenty of examples of characters who express themselves quite well without dialogue.

Creating Facial Expressions

Facial expressions convey a lot of emotion, and it's very important to understand these expressions and the way the face communicates emotion. When building an expression, always ask yourself what the character is feeling at the moment; this will help guide you to create the correct face.

Basic Expressions

The face can make an infinite number of expressions; luckily, most of them fall into some broad categories: anger, disgust, fear, joy, sadness, surprise. We'll detail these categories here, but you must recognize that they are only the extremes—primary colors among the many possible hues of expression. You could never animate with these six expressions alone, but understanding these basic "faces" can take you a long way toward understanding the underlying mechanics of facial expression.

Anger: The eyes are open, but the brows are down. The mouth is usually open, with the lips tensed and teeth bared. The jaw may be lowered.

Disgust: The whole face is tightened, with the eyes narrowed and the center brow lowered slightly. The mouth is closed and the upper lip pulled into a sneer.

Fear: The mouth is wide open and pulled back at the lower corners. The jaw is dropped, and the eyes are wide, with the brows raised.

Joy: The mouth is pulled upward into a smile, exposing the upper teeth and forcing the cheeks up. The brows are usually relaxed.

Sadness: The mouth is pulled down at the lower corners and may expose the lower teeth. The eyes squint and, when crying, may be closed. The brow is raised only in the middle.

Surprise: The eyes are wide open, and the brows are raised but not furrowed. The mouth is relaxed, and the jaw is slack.

The Upper Face

The upper part of the face is the most important part of an expression. If you want to change the meaning of an expression, look here, to the eyes and brows. The position of the brow probably conveys more information about emotion than any other part of the face. When the brows are lowered, it usually indicates a dark emotion, like anger. When the brows are raised, the face opens up. The eyes can also affect the meaning of an expression—looking away from a person can indicate shyness, for example.

Symmetry

When you're animating the face, it's always best to introduce asymmetry into the poses to make things look more natural. As with body posing, the dreaded "twins" can creep into facial animation, making your character's face look stale and boring. Still, you need to be careful not to make things too asymmetrical or it will change the meaning of the expression.

When the face pose becomes extremely asymmetrical, the expressions become less clear. If a character flashes a crooked smile, for example, it usually means he's not sincere. If one eyebrow is raised, it can indicate curiosity or insight. (Of course, if your character needs to express such emotions, this knowledge can work to your advantage.)

Changing the brow changes emotion. With his brows raised, the character looks happy.

With the same mouth but lowered brows, he looks evil.

A simple change in the eyes can also affect expression.

Complex Expressions

The palette of human emotions contains many subtle hues, and most expressions are not as distinct as the ones we've looked at up to now. Facial expressions are often asymmetrical, and they frequently combine various attributes of the basic expressions. A smiling mouth with lowered brows might indicate evil, for example.

When creating these expressions, remember the basics you learned from the fundamental expressions. Since the eyes are the most important in conveying emotion, start with them. As with the hips when posing the body, if you get the eyes right, the rest of the pose falls into place. If you ever get confused as to what the expression should be, make the face you want in front of a mirror and try to have the character mimic your own expression.

This face is symmetrical.

Lowering one side of the smile a bit introduces asymmetry and makes the face more natural.

Many complex expressions can be made out of the basic facial expressions.

Lower it too much, however, and the meaning of the expression changes.

Animating Facial Expressions

Understanding the basic expressions is a good start, but eventually you'll want to make the face move. All of the basic principles of animation that you learned while animating the body, like anticipation, overlap, and follow through, still apply.

One big reason morphing is used in facial animation is that it gives you the ability to overlap the actions of the face. Like motion in the body, facial actions do not happen all at once. A character may need to smile as he's talking, for instance, or change the position of his brows.

You may want to let one side of the face lead the other. If a character smiles, the left side of the face may begin the smile a frame or two ahead of the right. Also, as in head turns, the eyes tend to take the lead in facial animation. If the mood changes, the change usually begins with the expression of the eyes.

The audience needs to be watching the face when it undergoes a significant change of expression. In these situations, pose the character so that its face is clearly visible to the audience, and keep the character in that pose while

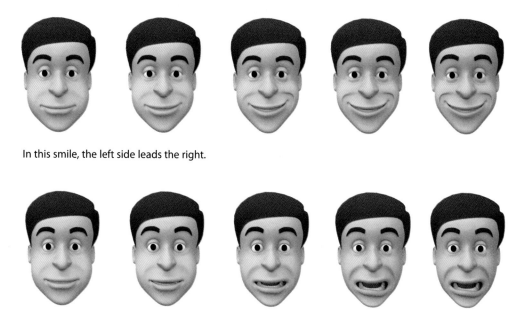

In this smile, the left side leads the right.

In this look of surprise, the upper face leads the lower.

the expression changes. If the body moves too much, its motion will over-whelm the action of the face, and if the head moves too much, the audience cannot see the face at all.

Animating the Head

As you begin animating the face, you will also need to study the head and how it moves. A perfectly animated face on a perfectly still head looks hor-rible. Head motions are necessary to accent and emphasize the facial ani-mation. If a character is talking, his head will nod or bob to accent certain lines of dialogue. If a character is curious, he may cock his head to one side. If the character is disapproving, the head may shake as if to say "no." If a character turns his head, it usually suggests a shift of attention or focus.

Remember the basic principles of animation: If a character turns his head to the right, he will anticipate it with a slight turn to the left. The character may also overshoot the turn slightly and then settle in.

An animated face on a perfectly still head is lifeless.

Head and body motions are needed to bring your character to life.

Animating the Eyes

Since the eyes are the most important part of the face, the direction in which the eyes point is also important. Be sure to have your character's eyes firmly fixed on the subject at hand—if your character is talking to someone but the eyes are looking off into the distance, your character will appear to be staring into space and not paying attention. Of course, this can be used as an effect, but typically you want your characters to be looking at the people they're talking to. Another little tidbit on human interaction is that even when a person moves his head slightly—to accentuate a part of speech, for example—the eyes tend to remain fixed on their target.

Blinks and Head Turns

During a head turn, most people tend to blink. Adding a blink into your character's head turns will make him seem more alive. Characters also tend to look in the direction of the head turn, so it's best to lead the turn with the eyes: if the head is turning left, the eyes will look left before the head turns.

Blinks and Eye Direction

One problem that often crops up is a character with a lazy eye that seems to float rather than locking onto a specific target. Some of these problems stem from poor eye direction, while others can be fixed with a simple blink. When people change the direction of their gaze, it is almost always accompanied by a blink. If your character looks from left to right, add a blink as the eyes change direction. The blink will help the eyes look less "floaty" and will also draw attention to the change in focus.

There are times when a character's eyes need to travel without blinking. One good example is when a character is reading, when the eyes go from left to right without a blink. Like the head, the eyes move along arcs, dipping slightly in the middle of a turn.

The eyes usually point in the direction of the head turn, and a blink in the middle adds some life.

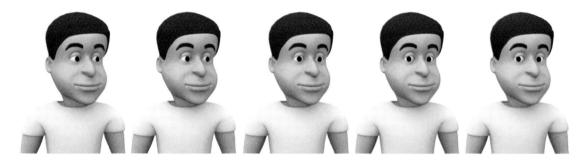

With no blink, this change in eye direction appears floaty.

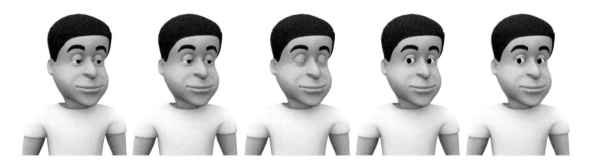

Adding a blink gives it more purpose and eliminates the float.

Eye Direction and Thought

There is a whole area of research that maps people's thoughts to the directions in which their eyes move. While this is just a theory, psychologists, among others, use this information to find visual cues as to how people think. Try remembering what you had for breakfast without moving your eyes. It's hard, right? Each thought that goes through a person's head triggers an unconscious motion in the eyes, and these motions can actually be mapped and used to the animator's advantage. While the exact motion of the character's eyes will depend on a wide range of stimuli, these rules of thumb can help guide you when animating a character's eyes.

The level of the eye also plays a role in the thought process. Eyes looking up indicate visual thoughts. A character looking up and to the left is remembering an image. Looking up and to the right means he is constructing an image.

The middle levels are associated with sound. Eyes looking directly left mean that a character is remembering something that was said. Looking right would mean he is constructing a new sentence.

The lower levels deal with emotion. Eyes looking diagonally down to the left indicate an internal dialogue, such as when difficult emotions are held inside. Emotions are expressed externally when a person looks diagonally down to the right.

Typically, eye motion to the left means the character is remembering something. Eye motion to the right means the character is constructing something new. This may mean he's thinking out a problem, or it could also mean that he is fabricating a lie or that the character is simply confused or guessing.

Making Eye Contact

The most important aspect of animating the eyes is keeping eye contact focused on the object of interest. If the character's eyes appear to be looking elsewhere, the character looks distracted or spaced out.

Eye contact is a tricky thing, however. The next time you're in a conversation, try to notice how often you make eye contact. Usually, it is only a fraction of the time. In fact, if someone stares at you constantly while talking, it appears abnormal.

Breaking eye contact is as important as making it. If a character becomes embarrassed or evasive, it tends to look away. Confident people usually make frequent eye contact when talking to others. On a related note, nervous and surprised people can be wide-eyed, whereas untrustworthy and defensive people often squint and dart their eyes from left to right.

Psychologists have discovered that infants are very sensitive to eye direction, so some of this awareness may be hard-wired into our brains. Among social species, eye direction indicates where another individual is looking and what that individual's future actions might be.

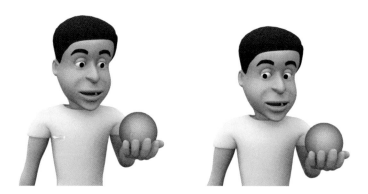

Eye direction is important. The audience will tend to look at whatever the character is looking at.

The lids should usually be kept slightly relaxed so that they can open wider.

Eyelids

Eyelids are most commonly used for blinking. Characters should blink every once in a while just so that they look alive. Blinks can also be used to great effect to draw attention to the character's face, such as in a change of eye direction.

When animating the eyelids, the first instinct is to keep the lids fully open so that the character seems alert. If you keep the lids 100 percent open, however, you can't open them wider, such as when the character is shocked or surprised. It is better to keep the "normal" lid of the character somewhere around 80 percent open instead. This keeps the character alert, but in a relaxed way. Plus, it gives you some flexibility for opening the eyes wider.

Warm personalities open the eyes wider, which can also be a sign of intelligence or attentive listening. These open communicators make use of "smiling eyes"; in the most extreme cases, a smiling cheek will lift so high that it affects the lower outline of the eye, pushing it up into a crescent or smiling eye. In contrast, an angry person may stare with squinted eyes for an uncomfortable length of time. It has also been discovered that people close their eyes briefly before giving a false answer.

Pupils

Dilation of the pupils is one area that is often overlooked when animating a character. In a realistic scene, pupil dilation from moment to moment is usually very subtle, but it can go a long way to indicate mood. Think of the scene in *Jurassic Park* where the T. rex looks in the window of the car and the pupil contracts when the flashlight beam hits it. The motion of the eye itself is what kept the character from appearing to be a giant puppet. This is an extreme example, and the size of the pupil usually remains fairly constant within a scene, changing between scenes as the character's mood and environment change.

Typically, the bigger the pupil, the more innocent and childlike a character seems. A character with small pupils seems to have "beady" eyes and appears to be less trustworthy. The quality of light in the scene also affects the pupils. More light results in smaller pupils; less light results in bigger pupils. If a character is dying of thirst in a sun-parched desert, make sure his pupils match the situation.

Animating Dialogue

Animating dialogue can really frighten the beginning animator, and rightly so, because it is one of the most difficult techniques for an animator to master. Like any hard task, however, animating dialogue is grounded in some very simple techniques—in this case, matching the character's mouth to the audio track and then animating the entire character to match.

Animating Lip Sync

The first step in animating dialogue is to sync the mouth to the dialogue track. This is called lip sync. Lip sync involves moving the lips to match an audio track by reading the audio track a frame at a time and then animating the character's mouth so that it speaks in rhythm with the track.

In animation, dialogue is almost always recorded before the characters are drawn. Dialogue looks more natural when the animator follows the natural rhythms of speech. Voice actors will have difficulty matching previously animated dialogue and still sounding natural, which is why recording the speech before animation begins is essential.

The animator is responsible for breaking down the dialogue track frame by frame into individual phonemes to be animated. This process is known as reading the track. The easiest way to picture a phoneme is to think of each discrete sound that makes up a word. The word "funny" for example has four phonemes: the "f" sound, the "uh" sound, an "n" sound, and finally, a long "ee." Reading a dialogue track can be a tedious task, as you'll have to break down the dialogue frame by frame. Computer animators have the advantage of using digital audio software to help them visualize their dialogue tracks.

The word "funny" contains four phonemes.

F   uh   n   eee

The Eight Basic Mouth Positions

In order to animate speech, you must first understand how the mouth moves when it speaks. Dozens of different mouth shapes are made during the course of normal speech. Animators usually boil these down to a handful of standard shapes that are used repeatedly. Depending on the style of animation, some animators get away with as few as three or four shapes, and some may use dozens. For most situations, you can get away with approximately eight basic mouth positions. These eight positions usually provide adequate coverage and give you the ability to animate most dialogue effectively.

To really see how these positions work, watch yourself in the mirror while you talk. Make the sounds used by each position. If you talk naturally, you'll begin to see how the shapes work and how they all fit together into a continuous stream. The shapes and the rules that govern them are certainly not strict. Different accents and speech patterns may cause you to substitute one shape for another in order to achieve a more convincing look.

You may notice that some of these positions are not in the standard library of shapes you modeled as morph targets. They can, however, be created as separate targets or created at animation time by mixing the appropriate sliders. One good example is the sound "oh," which is created by mixing an open jaw with the "ooo" sound. In fact, for speech, most of the grunt work is done by manipulating only these two shapes, with a possible "ffff" thrown in when needed. Other sliders, such as the smile, frown, and sneer, are used mainly to add character to the face.

Position 1 is the closed mouth used for consonants made by the lips, specifically the *M, B,* and *P* sounds. In this position, the lips are usually their normal width. For added realism, you could mix in an additional shape to get the lips slightly pursed, for sounds following an "ooo" sound, such as in the word "room."

Position 2 has the lips open with the teeth closed. This position is a common shape and is used for consonants made within the mouth, specifically the sounds made by *C, D, G, K, N, R, S, TH, Y,* and *Z.* All of these sounds can also be made with the teeth slightly open, particularly in fast speech.

Position 3 is used for the wide-open vowels such as *A* and *I.* It is essentially the same as the fundamental shape for an open jaw.

Position 4 is used primarily for the vowel *E,* but it can also be used on occasion for *C, K,* or *N* during fast speech.

Position 5 has the mouth wide open in an elliptical shape. This is the position used for the vowel *O,* as in the word "flow." It is created by mixing together an open jaw and the "ooo" sound. Sometimes, particularly when the sound is at the end of a word, you can overlap this shape with the one in position 6 to close the mouth.

Position 6 has the mouth smaller but more pursed. It is used for the "oooo" sound, as in "food," and for the vowel *U.* It is one of the fundamental mouth shapes.

Position 7 has the mouth wide open with the tongue against the teeth. This position is reserved for the letter *L.* It can also be used for the *D* or *TH* sounds, particularly when preceded by *A* or *I.* It is essentially an open jaw with the tongue moved up against the top teeth. If the speech is particularly rapid, this shape may not be necessary, and you can substitute position 2.

Position 8 has the bottom lip tucked under the teeth to make the sound of the letters *F* or *V.* In highly pronounced speech, this shape is necessary, but the shape could also be replaced with position 2 for more casual or rapid speech. This shape is one of the extra shapes modeled previously.

Reading the Track

Now that you understand the basic mouth positions, it's time to break down the track. If you have animator's exposure sheet paper, use it. Otherwise, get a pad of lined paper on which to write your track, using one line per frame. Load the dialogue into a sound editing program. A number of sound editing packages are available, and you should choose one that enables you to display the time in frames, as well as select and play portions of the track. The ability to label sections in the editor is also handy.

The first thing you should do is match your sound editing program's timebase to the timebase you're animating—30, 25, or 24 frames per second, for example. After your timebase is set, selecting a snippet of dialogue should enable you to listen to the snippet and read its exact length in the editor's data window. The visual readout of the dialogue gives you clues as to where the words start and stop. Work your way through the track, and write down each phoneme as it occurs on your exposure sheet, frame by frame. This is a tedious but necessary chore.

Some packages give you the ability to play back audio in sync with the animation. This feature is particularly helpful because you may be able to skip the step of reading the track and just eyeball the sync. Still, it's always a good idea to have read the track methodically before animating so that you completely understand it and know exactly where all the sounds occur.

You can use audio editing programs to read dialogue tracks.

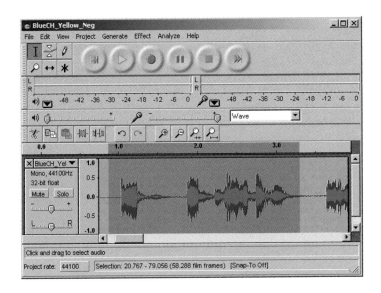

When reading the track, be sure to represent the sounds accurately. In human speech, most consonants are short and usually don't take up more than one or two frames. Vowels, however, can be of any length. If a person is shouting, for instance, you may have vowels topping 30 frames in length. In these cases, it is important that you don't simply hold the mouth in the exact same position for more than a second; it would look unnatural. Instead, create two slightly different mouth positions and keep the mouth moving between them so that the character looks alive.

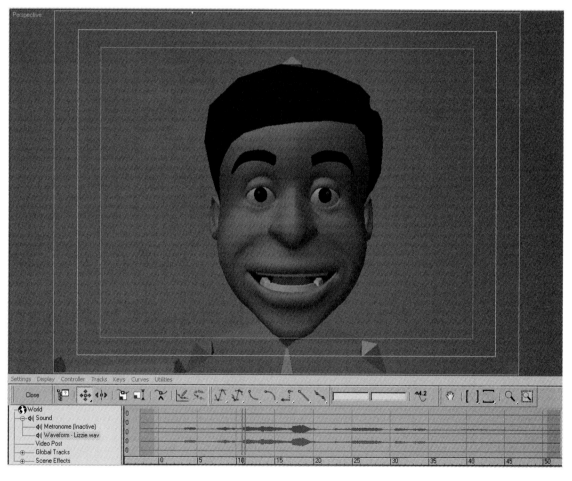

Most advanced 3D applications also allow you to view audio as you animate.

Animating the Mouth

Once you've read the track properly, the phonemes and their locations are pretty much known, and you can simply adjust the morph sliders to match the dialogue. While it may sound easy, the actual task of creating convincing lip sync is an art; not only does the character's mouth have to match the dialogue, it must also be fluid and seamless. Success requires practice and experience, but there are a few rules of thumb.

If the lips are generally in sync, the audience accepts the character. If the lips are out of sync, the audience senses that something is wrong. Lips that are overanimated also stand out like a sore thumb.

Vowels are the points in speech at which the mouth opens. When animating a vowel, you need two positions: The first position is the accent pose, when the vowel is first uttered. The second position is the cushion pose, which happens toward the middle to the end of the vowel sound. The accent usually has the mouth open wider than the cushion. One good way to do this is to animate the jaw so that it closes slightly as the vowel progresses. For fast vowels that happen over only two frames, this may not be much of an issue, but this rule applies to anything that takes four frames or more.

Consonants occur when the mouth closes. With the possible exception of a long M, F, or V sound, most consonants are only a few frames in length, and some can be less than one frame long. With this in mind, leave each position on the screen long enough for the audience to read it. Consonants must be on the screen for at least two frames in order to be read. If the consonant is too short, steal time from a vowel or combine two consonants into one.

When animating a vowel, you open the mouth quickly and close it slowly.

The best way to achieve smooth mouth motion is to concentrate on phrases rather than individual phonemes. An extreme example is rapid dialogue. In this case, the phonemes occur more frequently than once per frame. Animating even at one phoneme per frame makes the character's mouth appear to strobe or stutter. Typically, you should keep most mouth poses on the screen for at least two frames so that they are readable, so if the dialogue is more rapid than two phonemes per frame, you'll need to approximate the track by picking the most dominant phoneme. Vowels are always the loudest and longest sounds. Even when you're working with the fastest dialogue, accent the vowels.

One of the most common mistakes in animating the mouth is to create the phoneme shapes and let the computer do the inbetweens. This winds up looking incredibly mechanical. Just like motions of the body, motions in the face need to overlap. If you're animating your mouth shapes using muscle-based morph targets, you can adjust the curves slightly so that the motions overlap by a frame or two. This smooths out the mouth motion, so that the resulting animation looks more natural.

Another mistake is using a single set of stock phoneme shapes for all of a character's lip sync. This will provide no variety in the mouth shapes, which will make the character look mechanical.

As with overlap, muscle-based morph targets can help a lot. Go back over the animation and mix up the curves. If the character has a loud vowel sound, open the jaw more. Add some asymmetry by turning up the smile on one side of the face. In general, do whatever it takes to make the mouth match the character of the dialogue track on any given frame.

Consonants break up the vowels and are usually shorter in length.

Animating the Character

Lip sync gets the mouth to move, but dialogue involves the whole character, not just the face and mouth. When a character in a film is speaking dialogue, the audience sees an entire character composed of a body, arms, legs, and a head. Although the mouth is important, it is usually small in relation to the entire character. While the lips should be synced, much more important to the audience is the movement of the body and head, as well as the expression in the face and eyes. This is where you truly bring the character to life.

Mouth or Body First?

With the body so important to dialogue, one of the questions you might have is whether to animate the mouth or the body first. In cel animation, animators are forced to draw the mouths last, since it makes no sense the draw mouths on a character until the animation of the body is drawn. In stop motion, the mouths are done at the same time as the body. In computer graphics, it's really not that big of an issue, because any part of the animation can be tweaked independently of the others.

Some animators do the mouth first just to get the tedious task out of the way. It also is easier to get the mouth animated first on a still head rather than one that is moving. Other animators like to concentrate on the body first, and then get to the mouth. Both approaches work equally well, and since you can always go back and tweak the body and the lips independently, where you start is up to you.

Listening to the Track

Before you animate the character's body, you need to listen to the dialogue track—not for phonemes, but for mood. As you listen, close your eyes and try to picture yourself as the character. Pretty soon, you'll have an idea of what the character should be doing as the dialogue is spoken. This is where acting really enters the picture—you'll need to place yourself in the character's frame of mind to understand how the character will act.

As you listen, you'll also get a sense of the rhythm of the track. Certain words are emphasized more than others; note these on your script, because these are the major beats of the dialogue. Your character's major gestures usually happen near the beats, and this process gives you the timing of your animation. After you have the poses and the timing, you can begin to block out the animation, pose to pose.

Blocking Out Poses

The best way to animate dialogue is using standard pose-to-pose animation techniques, as outlined in Chapter 5. Posing to a dialogue track is like creating a dance to the spoken word instead of to music. Listening to the track will suggest a string of poses; try to make each one flow into the next. Once you have a mental picture of your character speaking the dialogue, you can thumbnail the poses or create them in the computer. A library of stock poses can help a lot with this process.

Keep your animation simple and direct. Try to animate one motion and emotion at a time. In any given frame, the character will have one thought and emotion going through its head, so illustrate that single thought in that single frame.

When you animate to dialogue, the timing of the track is fixed, so don't try to squeeze too many poses into this fixed amount of time. A pose generally needs at least 6 to 12 frames minimum to be read by the audience, but most poses will be held longer. To keep the number of poses under control, hit the major beats of the track first and then, if the animation needs more, fill in the holes with secondary poses.

A sequence of poses for a line of dialogue.

Timing the Poses

Once you have your poses blocked out, you need to sync them to the track. Find the major beats of the track and adjust the poses so that they "hit" a few frames before the beat. A thought manifests itself in the motions of the hands and body before it is voiced: think of a character who's having a difficult time saying something, perhaps a confession of love. As he searches for the right thing to say, his hands reveal the thought several seconds before he spits the words out—this is true even in normal conversation.

The body usually antici-pates the dialogue by a few frames.

Finishing the Animation

Once you've blocked out the basic poses, you can finish the rest of the animation using standard animation principles. When a character moves from one pose to the next, for example, he must anticipate the change and over-shoot the final pose before settling in. In addition to the main poses, dialogue animation requires a lot of secondary gestures and poses. These little details are what add life to the character.

Eyes and Dialogue

The eyes can add a whole new level of meaning to a line of dialogue.

When animating eyes with dialogue, be sure you understand where the character needs to be looking. Ask yourself who the character is talking to, and try to keep the eyes focused on the subject.

Of course, there are also places where a character may need to look away. People who are nervous tend to give darting glances. A dishonest person's eyes may be somewhat shifty. Don't be afraid to change the shape of the eyes and brows as the dialogue requires. A character whose eyes remain the same shape throughout a line of dialogue will appear lifeless.

Blinks are also very important. They accompany most major head motions, so if the head turns or bobs to accent a phrase, blink the eyes as well. Dead spots in the dialogue are also good places to sprinkle in a blink or two.

Head Motion and Dialogue

The head moves quite a bit when people talk, bobbing, nodding, and shaking to emphasize certain words. When your character makes a loud sound, it usually raises its head to help open the throat, and this is helpful to keep in mind when you're animating loud sounds or emphasis in speech.

When a character starts speaking, the head and body lift four to six frames before the mouth starts talking. This happens partly because the character needs to take a breath before talking. Lifting the character helps emphasize the start of speech and also draws the audience's attention to the character.

When animating a beat in which the head rises, it's always a good idea to anticipate the motion by lowering the head three or four frames before the accent, then popping the head up on the accented syllable. This is also known as a head bob, and it is usually accompanied by a blink. To get more action into the head bob, you can also involve the body: As the head moves down in anticipation of the accent, raise the shoulders a bit. When the head pops up, lower the shoulders. Taken to an extreme, this type of motion is the same as is used in the classic cartoon "take."

When a character shouts, its head tilts up to open the throat.

Hand Gestures and Dialogue

When talking, many people use their hands to clarify and emphasize the major points of their speech. Getting this part of the animation correct is a lesson in acting. If you want to see how *not* to animate the hands, watch some really nervous or first-time actors. They usually are very self-conscious and stuff their hands in their pockets, wring them nervously, or hang them loose at their sides.

In real life, body language precedes the dialogue by anywhere from a few frames to as many as 20. Generally, a slow, dim-witted character has more time between his gestures and his dialogue than a sharp, quick character. Speedy Gonzales has considerably less lead time in his gestures than Forrest Gump. Someone giving a long, boring speech will be much slower than a fire-and-brimstone evangelist.

You should also make an effort to ensure that your gestures fit the dialogue smoothly. The first gesture every animator learns is the ubiquitous finger point for emphasis, followed soon after by the fist pounding into the palm. These gestures certainly have their place, but within a much larger palette. As with most types of motions, simply watching people in their natural habitat is always your best reference.

Little details like hand gestures can add life to an animation.

Facial Animation

This first exercise will get you familiar with creating facial animation. Using a character that has been rigged for facial animation, do a series of tests that make the character go through a range of emotions:

- Make the character go from happy to angry.

- Make the character go from surprised to sad.

- Make the character go from disgusted to fearful.

Although the face will play an important part in depicting these emotions, you should animate the entire character. As the character goes from one emotion to the next, he will anticipate the change. The animation may include a breakdown pose to help guide the transitions.

Dialogue Animation

Now that you're comfortable animating facial expressions, move on to animating dialogue. For this exercise, find about 10 seconds of dialogue and animate your character speaking the line. You can record your own voice or have an actor record the line. If you don't have recording facilities, take a line from a movie or TV show and animate to that.

Make sure you read the track first, and then animate the lip sync. Once the mouth is in sync, animate the basic poses to match the track. Flesh out the animation with additional gestures and poses.

Conclusion

This chapter has discussed the fundamentals of facial and dialogue animation. The basics are easy to understand and grasp, but getting your animations to look good requires a lot of time, study, and practice. Always put your characters first, and keep their actions true to what they'd do in the real world.

CHAPTER EIGHT

Animal Motion

Animals are quite common in animation. Animators often need to bring non-human creatures to life. The anatomy of most four-legged mammals, as well as that of reptiles, dinosaurs, snakes, and insects, is quite different from our primate podiatry. This chapter gives you the essentials you need to animate most of the major types of animals.

Each animal has different ways of moving, depending on the creature's size, shape, and purpose. Small animals tend to move faster than large ones; predators move differently than prey. When animating animals, it is always a good idea to go to the source, so to speak, and get lots of reference for your animation. A trip to the zoo or a good nature documentary can help you understand how a particular animal moves.

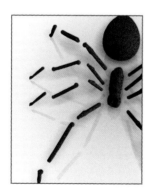

Four-Legged Mammals

The skeleton of a four-legged mammal is similar to the skeleton of a human in that they both have four limbs, and those limbs contain the same number of bones, not counting hands, feet, or paws. The lengths and arrangements of the bones are where the differences lie.

Take a dog, for example. Whereas humans walk on their heels and toes, the dog walks only on its toes. The dog's "heel" is far above the ground, approximately where a human knee would be. The dog's "knee" is actually even higher up, as are the thighs and hips. The front legs are similar to our arms, but again, the dog walks on its fingers. Like the heel, the dog's "wrist" is far above the ground, with the elbow even higher.

Heavy-set animals, like the hippo, appear to have short, stubby legs, because the animal's skin hangs lower and obscures the upper part of the leg. A hippo's skeleton looks much like the skeleton of any other four-legged creature, except that the upper parts of the legs are hidden inside the body.

The center of gravity is also slightly different for a four-legged beast. Rather than being located at the hips, it is farther up on the body, roughly centered between the front and back legs. The center of gravity is important in animation. If the animal were to leap, for example, the entire body's rotation would center around this point. An animal such as a dachshund has a center

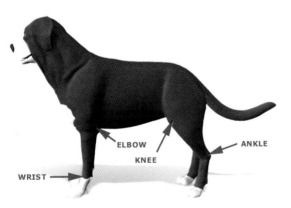
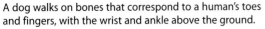

A dog walks on bones that correspond to a human's toes and fingers, with the wrist and ankle above the ground.

A hippo's elbows and knees are located near the belly, and the upper parts of its legs are hidden under its heavy skin.

of gravity near the middle of the spine. Other animals, like chee-
tahs and greyhounds, have large chests, which places the center of
gravity farther forward on their bodies. The head also plays a role
in determining the center of gravity. A giraffe's long neck places
its center of gravity farther up the spinal column, at the back of
the shoulders.

The center of gravity is
usually located halfway
between the hips and
shoulders.

Skeletons for Quadrupeds

A quadruped is any animal that has four legs, and quadruped skeletons are
fairly easy to build. A quadruped skeleton is similar to a human skeleton:
the animal has hips and shoulders connected via a spinal column, but
the spine is aligned horizontally rather than vertically. Another factor to
consider is that the bones of the limbs are not the same length as those of
humans.

The hierarchy of a quadruped's body is usually constructed like that of a
bipedal character, with the root of the hierarchy at the hips. Some people,
however, like to rig the root a little farther forward, such as at the middle of
the spine, which is closer to the animal's actual center of gravity. This decision is really a matter of taste, and either way will work fine.

A quadruped skeleton is similar to a human skeleton but is
aligned horizontally rather than vertically.

Inverse kinematic (IK) chains are the best way to build the
legs.

An animal's tail can be created by using a simple chain of bones.

Most four-legged mammals also have tails. A tail is easy to configure as a simple chain of linked bones connected to the hips. These are typically animated using forward kinematics.

To keep the animation simple, some animators like to tie the many bones of a tail to a single set of sliders that control the bones' rotations. This is as easy as linking the rotation of each bone to a slider. Moving one slider rotates many bones.

Analysis of a Four-Legged Walk

Most four-legged mammals, particularly cats and dogs, walk with their legs moving in opposition, much as the hips and shoulders move in a human walk: when the right rear foot is forward, the left right foot is back. The creature's legs still rock back and forth at the hips, but the upper body motion is parallel to the ground rather than perpendicular to it. Whereas human shoulders rock back and forth on the vertical axis, a dog's "shoulders" rock back and forth on a horizontal axis as the front legs move back and forth. There are, however, a few exceptions. Giraffes, bears, and camels, to name a few, move their legs a side at a time, so that both the right rear leg and the right front leg move forward at the same time.

To maintain balance in a four-legged walk, the animal will usually walk with the front and rear legs slightly out of phase. This means when the front legs are passing each other, the rear legs are extended. This allows the animal to keep three of the four feet on the ground for a moment to create a stable, balanced platform. In the language of the horseman, a walk is considered a "four-beat" gait. This means that in a single walk cycle, each foot will hit the ground at a different time:

Beat 1—right rear leg

Beat 2—right front leg

Beat 3—left rear leg

Beat 4—left front leg

As the legs move forward through the step, the legs that are not currently planted on the ground (the free legs) move forward. At this point, the spine is straight when viewed from the top, but may bow or arch a bit more when viewed from the side.

The legs then move through the step and the free feet strike the ground, repeating the first step.

In this step, the right rear foot is about to strike the ground.

Halfway through the step, the free legs are moving forward. Notice how the front leg's joint causes a different bend in the leg than that of the rear.

Other Four-Legged Gaits

In addition to the walk, a four-legged animal can have several other gaits: the trot, the canter, and the gallop. The animal varies the timing and rhythm of its steps as it moves faster and faster. By the time the creature has reached full gallop, the front legs are in sync, going forward and back nearly in unison, with the back legs operating as a mirror to the front.

Trot

The trot is a two-beat gait—the feet hit twice during one cycle. The animal's legs move in diagonal pairs, with the animal airborne for a few frames between each stride and diagonal pairs of feet hitting the ground at the same time. Another way to view this is that when the left front leg is fully back, the left rear leg is forward, and vice versa. The animal holds its head higher at a trot than it does at a walk, and the head remains almost still along the vertical axis.

In a trot, the feet hit in this order:

Beat 1—right front/left rear

Beat 2—left front/right rear

During a trot, the animal's legs move in diagonal pairs, with the animal airborne for a few frames between each stride.

Canter

The canter is an asymmetrical three-beat gait, and can start with either the right or left leg. If the animal is cantering on its "right lead" (usually when it's turning to the right), the sequence is as follows: left rear leg goes forward, right rear and left front legs move forward together, and finally the right front leg moves forward. At this last stage, after the animal uses the right front foot to push off for the next stride, there is a period when all four feet are off the ground. This gait also causes the animal's body to rock back and forth as it moves.

This sequence shows a right-lead canter; a left-lead canter would mirror this sequence with the opposite feet:

Beat 1—left rear leg

Beat 2—right rear leg/left front leg

Beat 3—right front leg

The canter is the precursor to the gallop.

Gallop

In the gallop, the animal extends to its full reach and speed. The animal is in the air longer because there's a bigger launch, and the footsteps fall faster. The step sequence of a gallop is very similar to that of a canter—only faster and more stretched out. In fact, it's stretched out so much that it becomes a four-beat gait. Like the canter, the gallop can start on either side.

A "right-lead" gallop would be as follows:

> Beat 1—left rear leg
>
> Beat 2—right rear leg
>
> Beat 3—left front leg
>
> Beat 4—right front leg

The gallop is a four-legged creature's equivalent of a run.

Stylized Walks

The back legs on this dog are not realistic; they bend in the same way human legs do. Still, the cartoon nature of his design permits us to do this and get away with it.

Another way to view a four-legged walk is in a more cartoony way. Think of the old vaudeville act in which two guys get into a tattered old horse suit. In this case, the horse literally walks like two people stitched together. You animate the walk like a double two-legged walk. This forces you to have different joint constraints and body construction.

You can also stylize a four-legged walk by adding personality. Try to understand the character and its mood as you animate a walk. The mechanics of four-legged walks may be somewhat complex, but you can take the walk beyond mechanics. Even if the resulting walk is not quite real, if the animation looks good, the audience will accept it.

Reptiles

Quadrupedal reptiles, such as lizards and crocodiles, tend to keep their stomachs very close to the ground, with the legs splayed out to the side. With few exceptions, most four-legged reptiles have the same awkward position. This keeps the reptile's center of gravity quite low, making it more difficult to raise the body off the ground. In contrast, the legs of quadrupedal mammals are directly underneath the body, which allows the legs to carry all of the animal's weight and is more efficient.

A reptilian walk is similar to a mammalian walk in that the front and back legs move in opposition. The reptile's low center of gravity, however, forces the body to work more. As it walks, a reptile bends its torso into a curve to help push the feet along. Despite this awkward motion, some reptiles are capable of traveling at moderate speeds. Crocodilians raise their bodies off the ground and make short, fast rushes. Short-bodied lizards also can move fast for short distances. In fact, some lizards can lift their front legs off the ground when running. Longer-bodied lizards have greater difficulty in raising their bodies, because they have short legs. This forces their bodies to move more like snakes do. (If you remove a lizard's legs completely, the result is a snake.)

The legs of crocodiles, as well as those of lizards and other reptiles, splay out to the side.

In a reptilian walk, the reptile's low center of gravity forces the spine and torso to bend much more than a mammal's do.

Snakes

Snakes move in a unique way, and to the casual observer, it seems almost magical that an animal with no legs can move so quickly and gracefully. Snakes travel best on surfaces with obstructions and some roughness. This gives their bellies something to grip. Snakes do not do very well on slippery surfaces.

If you put a snake on loose sand, you can see that every part of its belly touches the ground, and it flows along in a series of S curves. On the back of each curve you can see that the sand has been pushed up. The body pivots and pushes sideways against these piles and is propelled forward. They swim in water with the same motion.

Snakes have several different modes of locomotion. The method a snake uses depends on several factors, such as its size, the roughness of the surface, and the speed of travel. Typically, the snake finds a bump or rough spot on the surface and pushes against that with its body to move forward.

Serpentine Locomotion

Serpentine locomotion uses the classic S curve and is the most common method of travel used by snakes. In lateral undulation, waves of sideways bending are propagated along the body from head to tail. The snake's muscles are activated sequentially along the body, relaxing and contracting to form an "S" shape. As the snake progresses, each point along its body follows the path established by the head and neck, like the cars of a train following the engine as it moves along the track.

Serpentine locomotion is the most common method of travel used by snakes. Each point of the body follows along the S-shaped path established by the head and neck, much like the cars of a train following the track.

Sidewinding

Sidewinding is used by many snakes to crawl on smooth or slippery surfaces. It is similar to lateral undulation in the pattern of bending but differs in a few ways. First, the snake's body doesn't slide along the ground; instead, it lifts part of the body while firmly setting down other parts. This allows the snake to get a better grip.

Next, the parts of the body that are not firmly planted on the ground are lifted up, causing the body to roll along the ground from neck to tail, forming a characteristic track.

Finally, because the snake repeatedly lifts parts of the body, it moves diagonally relative to the tracks it forms on the ground.

The distance that the snake lifts its body off the ground is usually measured in fractions of an inch, which is practically negligible from the audience's viewpoint. For added effect, you can exaggerate this lift when animating this type of motion.

In sidewinding, the snake actually lifts parts of the body and sets them down again.

Sidewinding causes the snake to move diagonally relative to the "S" shape.

Concertina Locomotion

With concertina locomotion, the snake alternately folds the body back and forth like an accordion and then lifts and straightens the body to move forward. The front part of the body then comes to rest on the surface and the back part is lifted and pulled up into the accordion shape again. Concertina locomotion is used mostly in crawling through tunnels or narrow passages and in climbing.

Rectilinear Locomotion

Rectilinear locomotion lets the snake move straight ahead with its body stretched out, or perhaps along a wide arc with its body slightly curved. This type of motion is used primarily by large snakes, such as boa constrictors and pythons. In rectilinear locomotion, the snake pulls its belly scales forward and lifts them off the ground, then sets them down and pushes backward. Because the scales are aligned like a ratchet, this pulls the snake forward.

Dinosaurs

Dinosaurs are a unique case because we do not have any direct reference as to how they moved. There are no videotapes or films of these creatures in their natural habitat. Many scientists have tried to decipher dinosaur locomotion from the fossil record, but their conclusions are always open to

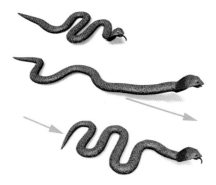

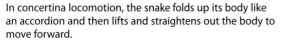

In concertina locomotion, the snake folds up its body like an accordion and then lifts and straightens out the body to move forward.

Rectilinear locomotion lets the snake move straight ahead with its body stretched out.

debate. Observations of similar animals that are still living give us the best motion reference. A four-legged dinosaur, such as a triceratops, would most likely have moved like a large four-legged modern animal, such as a hippo or rhinoceros.

Bipedal dinosaurs, such as a T. rex, are a bit more difficult to pin down, because no creatures alive today have bodies similar to theirs. To figure out how these dinosaurs moved, scientists have tried to reconstruct their walks and runs using sophisticated physical models. Movies like *Jurassic Park* have popularized one particular brand of locomotion, which is based to some degree on the scientific research into this subject. This style seems to make sense and is the one we will use.

The crux of this style is that the back legs of a two-legged dinosaur are much like those of a bird. In this style, the dinosaur walks on its toes, with the body generally upright. The long tail acts as a counterbalance, which allows the upper body to pivot freely at the hips. As the dinosaur walks, the hips pivot much as a human's do, but the tail also rotates a bit to compensate.

As a bipedal dinosaur begins to run, the shoulders drop significantly as the body stretches out. This allows the tail to extend and counterbalance the upper body, which makes the locomotion process more efficient.

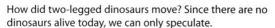

How did two-legged dinosaurs move? Since there are no dinosaurs alive today, we can only speculate.

One theory is that dinosaurs moved somewhat like birds because they were the ancestors of birds. As a bipedal dinosaur begins to run, the shoulders drop significantly as the body stretches out to maintain balance.

Insects and Spiders

Insects and spiders are fairly easy to animate. Because an insect is the quintessential segmented creature, you can build its parts separately and connect them together via a simple hierarchy. Shape animation or skeletal deformations are not needed for such a creature, because an insect's exoskeleton does not change shape. The one exception may be antennae on the insect, which can be animated with bones or, more directly, using a simple bend modifier.

Setting Up Insects for Animation

Even though your insects may not need to be deformed, it can be a good idea to use IK chains for the legs. An insect's legs are typically composed of three joints connected to the underside of the body. These three joints are the insect equivalent of our thigh, shin, and foot.

A simple three-joint IK chain for each leg makes animation much easier, because the only objects that need to be animated are the insect's feet and body. Legs can be built with the joints as separate segments. These can then be linked to the IK chains so that animation can take place. You can also build the legs as a single mesh, which must then be deformed.

Insects and spiders don't need to be deformed, unlike animals with skin.

This spider is built of simple segments.

An IK chain is used to manipulate the legs. The chains are then linked to the body via a hierarchy.

Analysis of Six-Legged Walks

If four-legged walks seem complex, you may think that a six-legged walk would be intolerably difficult. This, fortunately, is not the case. An insect walk actually follows a definite, repeatable pattern that can be animated fairly easily. A six-legged walk is very similar to a four-legged walk: The front two legs take a step forward with one foot and then the other. The second set of legs mirrors this motion. The third set of legs mirrors the second, closely matching the motion of the front legs, but slightly offset. Insects generally keep at least three legs on the ground, forming a stable tripod at all times.

Animating the walk of an insect is simply a matter of getting the front legs to walk, then mirroring this motion in the second set of legs, and finally mirroring the motion of the second set of legs in the third set. The legs of an insect have three main segments, with the first segment, closest to the body, acting like a suspension bridge that holds the body of the bug aloft.

Insect legs suspend the insect's body like a bridge.

Like the body of a two- or four-legged creature, the body of an insect bounces up and down as the creature walks. This rate of bounce is directly proportional to the rate of the walk. The body bounces up and down once per step—meaning that the insect bounces twice for a full cycle of right and left leg steps. The bug is highest when the legs are in the middle of the stride.

The rate of an insect walk depends on the species of bug and the bug's demeanor. Generally, bugs move pretty fast compared to mammals, and a quarter or eighth of a second per step is not out of the question. When walks get this fast, the frame rate of the animation becomes a limiting factor. At 24 feet per second, an eighth-second stride takes only three frames per step. This is about as fast as a walk can be animated, with one frame each for the forward, middle, and back portions of the step.

The legs are best dealt with a set at a time. The front legs are always a good guide, so these should be animated first. Once the front legs are moving, you can keyframe the rear sets of legs in the same manner. (The middle and rear sets of legs move in an identical manner as the front set, but are mirrored.) This makes creating the animation as simple as repeating the exact same steps you used to animate the front legs—creating a key for the beginning, middle, and end of each step—and then adjusting the inbetweens as required.

The insect's body moves up and down as it walks.

One tactic to use with the rear legs is to copy and paste the animation from the front legs to the corresponding rear legs. For this to work, the pivots of all the joints of the respective legs need to be aligned along the same axis. If they are not, the rotations do not translate properly, and the legs can't mirror the exact rotations of the front. To fix this, align all the pivots on the legs to the world axis before animation begins.

Another problem with copying animation may be one of scale. The cockroach, for example, has rear legs that are quite a bit longer than its front legs. Copied rotations from the front leg may not match up exactly. Another factor to consider is timing. If all three legs in motion were to lift on the exact same frame, the animation would look stiff and unnatural. To compensate for this, slide the keys for each set of legs back a frame or two so that they each lift slightly behind the leading legs. This adds an extra touch of realism.

One final thing to consider with insects is their antennae. These act as feelers for the insect, constantly searching out a path for the bug to follow. Antennae can be animated using a number of methods, such as bones with a mesh deformation system. A simple bend modifier can also be quite effective, because you can achieve a nice effect by keyframing the angle and direction of the bend.

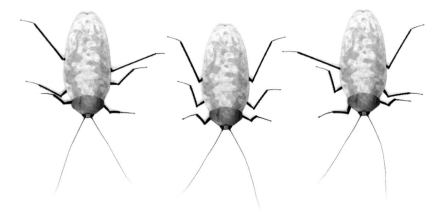

The extremes of an insect walk. When the right leg is forward, the left is back, and vice versa. Notice how each set of legs mirrors the position of the one in front of it.

Spider Walks

An eight-legged walk is similar to a six-legged walk, with an extra set of legs to manage. The fourth (rear) set of legs mirrors the rest.

Because a spider can easily support its body while walking on six legs, many times spiders use their front set of legs independently. Similarly to the way an insect uses its antennae to feel its way around, a spider may use its front legs to check out the road ahead. A spider can also use its front legs like arms to perform such tasks as spinning a web, or perhaps capturing dinner.

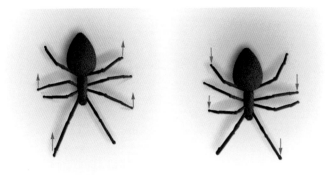

An eight-legged walk is similar to a six-legged walk, with an extra set of legs to manage.

Because a spider can easily support its body while walking on six legs, spiders often use their front legs independently.

Animating a Four-Legged Walk Cycle

A quadrupedal skeleton can be made to walk quite easily. It is a simple matter of getting the back legs to walk like a two-legged character's and then adding the front leg motions. When animating a four-legged walk, you need to ensure that both pairs of legs move the same distance with each step. If the back legs have a larger stride than the front legs, for example, the back of the creature will soon be ahead of the front.

The timing of the walk is important. As with the human walk, timing depends on a number of factors, including the size of the animal, the type of gait, and the animal's mood. Larger animals take more frames for each step—an elephant steps much more slowly than a mouse, for example. The animal's mood is also a big factor—a tired dog will walk much more slowly than a happy one.

In this exercise, you will use an IK skeleton to animate a simple four-legged walk. The timing will be one step every 12 frames.

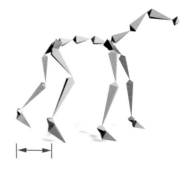

1. Start by positioning the back legs. Rotate the back hips and place the right back foot forward. Exactly how far forward depends on the animal; a creature with longer legs may step as far as halfway up the body.

2. Position the front legs by mirroring the pose on the back legs, placing the left front foot forward. This means that, for this step, the forward feet (left front and right rear) remain planted.

3. Both pairs of legs should have the feet approximately the same distance apart. This distance is the stride length. Take a note of this distance as a reference for the next step by estimating it or measuring it exactly.

4. Animate the first step. In a four-legged walk, you need to make sure both pairs of feet move the same distance. Move the time slider ahead to frame 12. Set keys for the feet that are currently forward (right front and left rear).

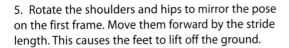

5. Rotate the shoulders and hips to mirror the pose on the first frame. Move them forward by the stride length. This causes the feet to lift off the ground.

6. Double the stride length to move the back feet forward, and then set a key. Scrubbing the animation produces a walk in which the feet only slide.

7. Go to the middle of the stride (frame 6) and create the middle pose. Lift the two legs that are moving forward off the ground.

8. As in a bipedal walk, lifting the legs throws the hips and shoulders out of balance slightly. Rotate the hips and shoulders so that the side with the moving leg is lower than the side with the planted leg.

9. Finally, the hips and shoulders also rise and fall vertically, much like a biped's hips. This is the key to implying the animal's weight. The recoil position, in which the body absorbs the weight of the planted foot, is at approximately frame 3 in this step. Move to that frame and lower both the hips and shoulders. At frame 6, they are at their peak. Move to that frame and lift the hips and shoulders so that the planted leg is at full extension.

10. Scrub the animation. This is just the first step. Repeat this procedure for each additional stride.

This gives you a basic walk. You might want to play with the timing of the feet, however, to give it a bit more realism. You can do this by offsetting the motion of opposite feet by a frame or two so that the feet don't hit at exactly the same time. Another trick is to add weight shifts for each step, which will help make the animation more realistic.

Conclusion

As you have seen, animals come in many sizes and shapes. Animating them does not need to be a complex task. Try to understand the way an animal moves, through research and reference. Once you have the basics, filter those motions through the personality of the animal to turn it into a character.

CHAPTER NINE

Acting

Animators are, in many respects, actors who use computers, pencils, or clay to bring a character to life—although while the actor works in front of an audience, the animator typically works alone, seeing the reaction of the audience only later. Bringing your character to life in a convincing manner means understanding the techniques of acting, such as being able to think and breathe like your character. When you truly step into a character, the actual act of animating becomes a bit of a blur. You become the conduit from the character to the mouse.

The animator makes characters communicate, not only with each other, but also with the audience. Characters must not only tell a story, they must also tell it in a believable and entertaining manner. When the audience pays for a ticket to your film, switches on your TV show, or downloads your movie from the Internet, they are expecting to be entertained, enlightened, and amused.

Acting Vs. Animating

Plenty of instructors and schools can teach you how to act, and these techniques can be of great value to an animator. As you become more involved with creating characters, you can draw upon many techniques from the art of acting.

Acting, however, is fundamentally different from animation. Acting happens in real time, usually in front of an audience. As a result, actors need to learn how to deal with the here and now. If a fellow actor flubs a line, a good actor is quick enough to cover the faux pas flawlessly. And actors cannot go back and fix a couple of frames; they have to re-create the entire performance.

Animation is a much more solitary pursuit. Most of the time it's just you and the computer. Animating is also like acting in slow motion—one frame at a time—and thus animators have the luxury of going back over a performance frame by frame until they consider it perfect.

The downside of going over the scene again and again is that there is a much higher chance of the scene appearing stale, forced, or over-thought. The only way to avoid this is to go with your gut when you first act out the scene and then to try to preserve that spontaneous vision throughout the process of animating and refining the scene. Some animators tend to thumbnail their poses as they act out the scene, because it is much faster and more spontaneous than blocking it out in a 3D package.

According to the most popular realistic school of acting, actors must work from the inside out—from motivation and emotion to physical action. If an actor consciously thinks about raising the eyebrows in surprise, for example, that action may appear forced. The action must come from an internal motivation, and once the emotion of surprise is achieved, the external expression (raising the eyebrows) will occur naturally.

The animator, on the other hand, works in exactly the opposite way. Animators must use externals to illustrate the internal, because the character being animated doesn't have internal emotions—it is simply a collection of bytes on the disk. The only way to communicate emotion to the audience is to change the external parts of the character to illustrate those emotions.

Thumbnailing poses on paper is a fast way to visualize a scene.

Acting and Story

The characters that you animate are the storytellers. They need to convey the script to the audience in a convincing and entertaining manner. The greatest story in the world can be ruined if it is told by a poor storyteller. To make the story jump off the screen, you need to understand the story, story structure, and how each scene moves the story forward.

Each scene has an objective, a point it needs to get across. Each character within the scene also has an objective. A policeman, for example, wants to take the criminal to jail. The criminal's objective is freedom. How these two objectives work out determines how the story progresses. If the criminal escapes, you have *The Fugitive*. If he goes to jail, you have a different story, such as *Cool Hand Luke*. When you animate a scene, be clear as to your character's objectives and how they affect the story.

You can also view the character's objective as a survival mechanism. Every character has a very primitive need to survive in the world, and most objectives are driven by the simple need to survive. If you understand that the policeman and the criminal are both simply trying to survive, you can clarify their actions and goals.

Know Your Tools

Acting is pure right-brain activity. You need to remain totally "in the moment" so that you can truly become one with your character. In a Zen sense, when you connect with the right side of the brain, your character flows through you and subconsciously takes control of the mouse. You don't have to think consciously about how a character is moving; it just moves. Posing in a 3D app is often too slow, and some animators resort to good, old-fashioned pencil and paper. Regardless of the medium, constantly stepping out of your creative frame of mind to solve technical problems or to consult the manual breaks the flow and can weaken your animation.

Before you ever start acting for animation, you need to master your chosen software tools: you should be able to set and modify keyframes automatically, without conscious thought. Your characters also need to be rigged properly so that they are rock solid and easy to manipulate. You don't want technical issues to crop up during animation that will break your creative flow.

In addition, a good knowledge of human motion, which is discussed elsewhere in this book, will help you remain in the moment. You should be able to construct natural, balanced poses without much effort. Thinking about the pose is a left-brain activity. Don't go there.

Know Your Audience

One thing that new animators tend to overlook is the audience. If you are animating for a Saturday morning children's show, your acting choices will probably be different than if you're animating for a late-night comedy show. Knowing your audience helps you create a performance that will be understood and accepted.

Don't, however, fall into the trap of letting the audience dictate the performance. Pandering is not allowed. Don't make obvious choices. If you do what the audience expects all the time, they become bored. Always think of taking the left turn when the audience expects you to veer right. What are you going to do in this performance to make it interesting and keep the audience entertained?

If a character goes to put a coin in a slot, the audience expects a simple motion, but you can step away from that expectation and make the action a little more memorable. Perhaps the character is a klutz and fumbles the coin. A suave character may toss the coin into the slot from a short distance. Little touches like this can help sell the character's personality to the audience.

Know Your Characters

The foundation of good acting is understanding who your character is and what makes him tick. If you truly know your character, you innately know how and when the character is going to move and how it reacts to the world. Gaining an understanding of a character can be a long and involved process, and actors use many techniques to accomplish this.

One method is to ask yourself some questions about your character. You need to ask about the basics, such as height, weight, age, gender, overall health, and so on. Knowing the character's personality, dreams, aspirations, and flaws are also important for this process.

Character Descriptions

To answer these questions, you can create a simple character description. The writer often does this as part of the writing process. If you are animating a one-shot character in a commercial, however, you may have to come up with your own description.

A character description is a paragraph or less, and goes over the basics of the character. Usually, it covers just the important features, such as age, sex, and basic personality. It can also go into other little details, such as the character's quirks and personality flaws.

Chester is a very young inventor with a large imagination. He loves to take stuff he finds around the house and turn it into just about anything he can dream up—spaceships, cars, catapults, and automatic dog ticklers. Once he makes something, Chester goes into his imagination, where he takes his dog, Orson, on wild adventures with his new inventions.

Orson is Chester's dog and constant companion. He follows Chester everywhere. Orson is always up for adventure and oftentimes will even lead the way. Sometimes Orson comes away from these adventures a little worse for wear, but he always recovers and has a constant smile on his face.

Character Biographies

A simple description is often fine for short-form projects, such as commercials and interstitials. If you are animating a longer-form project, however, such as a feature, you may want to create a more in-depth biography that really nails down the character's personality. On larger commercial projects, the writer will usually create a biography for the production to reference, but for your own films you'll need to do this work yourself.

A biography is more formal than a description and is usually a page or two in length. Like the description, it gives the basics of the character but with a lot more depth. It might go into a character's education, family, traumatic events, or anything else that has shaped the character's life.

Some people go totally overboard in a character biography, writing what amounts to a good-sized FBI file. For a feature film, this is probably a good idea, because the character needs to be as fleshed out as much as possible before animation begins. If your character is going to show up for 15 seconds in a malted-milk-ball commercial, though, you'll do just fine without knowing the names of the character's maternal grandparents.

For characters in a TV series, the biography is constantly evolving. Sometimes it's best not to lock things down, because the writers and animators invariably discover new things about the characters as the series progresses. When *Rocko's Modern Life* was pitched, there was no information about Heffer's parents. In the first season, Vince Calandra wrote a terrific story about how Heffer's parents were actually wolves, who adopted him with the plan of fattening him up for dinner. Instead of eating him, however, they fell in love with him. This episode was both funny and poignant, and it added a whole new dimension to Heffer's character, which was used in many subsequent episodes.

Acting Technique

Once you understand your character, you need to put that knowledge into action by acting and performing the character. Acting is an art form, and like any other art form, it has a number of core techniques. These techniques, however, are only the tip of the iceberg—as with any art form, the deeper you explore, the more there is to learn.

Creating Empathy

The big goal of an animator, as well as of the writers, is to create empathy for the character. Empathy means that the audience emotionally connects with the character on some level and identifies with him. This is not to be confused with sympathy, where the audience simply feels sorry for someone. When a character evokes sympathy, members of the audience say, "I pity that guy." When the audience feels empathy, however, they can say, "I know how that guy feels; I've been there myself." A character who evokes empathy plays to the heart.

Say that you need to animate the oldest gag in the book: a character slipping on a banana peel. You can have the character's feet fly out from under him and have him land on his rear end, then get up and move along. Pretty boring, and the audience will not feel much empathy for the character.

Instead, try to bring out your character by showing a side of his personality to the audience. This enables the audience to go beyond simply viewing the action to feeling what your character is feeling. If the character is an extremely dignified person, he might get up quickly and look around to make sure he didn't embarrass himself in front of others. If the character is starving to death, perhaps he'll pull the banana peel off the bottom of his shoe and eat it, turning an unfortunate incident into a humorous blessing.

Villains also need to generate empathy. How many times have you seen a cartoon in which the villain was completely evil, with no redeeming qualities? These villains are usually two-dimensional and not very interesting. Just like the hero, villains need to get the audience on their side. The scariest villains are the ones who appear real to the audience. A good villain is really just a character with a few fatal flaws. The evil character will still want many of the things normal people want, but his priorities are skewed. Darth Vader is a classic villain, yet he still wants his son Luke to follow in his footsteps—just as many fathers do.

Think of Kathy Bates in *Misery*. She created a very real and very scary character. Most people know someone who is a big fan of an actor, a TV series, a movie, or the characters in a series of books, as in this case. When Kathy Bates's character learns that an author (played by James Caan) is essentially going to kill her favorite book series (along with its characters), she does what she must to protect them. She detains James Caan's character and forces him to keep them alive by writing more books. It's almost as though it's her motherly duty to protect those characters. Even though her measures are extreme, the audience identifies with her, as both an ardent fan and a protective mother.

When you animate, try to get the audience to understand your character and what it is feeling. Go beyond the actions to dig deep into the character's personality and find actions that define your character.

Creating Inspiration

Animation is performing, and a good performance is an inspired performance. One starting point for creating inspiration is a concept the great acting coach Stanislavski (the originator of the modern style of realistic acting) described as the "magic if." The "magic if" asks the question "What would I do if I were in these circumstances?"

The answer to this simple question can be a springboard to creativity and inspiration. As an animator you get the chance to be someone else for the day—a fictional character, a cartoon. In a true cartoon world, what *would* you do if you had an anvil dropped on your head? For the cartoon character, this sort of stuff happens all the time and is perfectly normal. When you put yourself totally in the character's environment and circumstances, it inspires you.

In many respects, this technique is a lot like play-acting. A child truly believes her doll is real. It is the job of animators to make the digital props and sets real to themselves. By using the "magic if," animators grant themselves permission to "believe" in these imaginary objects.

In a true cartoon world, what would you do if you had an anvil dropped on your head? When you put yourself totally in the character's environment, it inspires you.

Creating Movement

Until a character moves, it is nothing but a nicely modeled mannequin. Animating a character and bringing it to life requires that you move it. The first thing a novice animator does is start moving body parts around to see what happens. This trial and error approach can have its moments, but a professional animator needs a much larger arsenal. First, you need to understand that characters always move for a reason. Those reasons are almost always emotionally driven. You cannot "will" emotions. In life, emotions result from stimuli, which affect the character's senses and evoke an emotional response.

The emotions the character feels dictate the type and quality of the motion: a sad character moves much differently than a happy one, for example. Being able to convey a character's emotions through motion is what makes an animator great.

Different emotions cause a character to move differently.

Most of the time, people do not think about the individual actions they perform. When you walk, you don't usually think about placing one foot in front of another—if you're in love, for example, you're thinking about your lover while you happen to be walking. The emotions dictate the character of the walking motions. When a comedian tells a joke, you laugh; you do not think, "Now I'm going to laugh." This is the key to good animation. Your character's movements need to be unforced and natural.

The best way to animate this sort of natural motion is to try to block out your poses quickly and develop a creative flow. You can do this by using a fast and easily manipulable rig, pulling up stored poses, or simply thumbnailing the poses on paper. When you are truly acting, you are not really thinking about the individual motions, and the same should happen when you start animating. As things start to flow creatively, each pose just happens as a consequence of the emotions your character is feeling. Once you've blocked these basic poses out, you can switch your brain over to a more technical mind-set and critically analyze your poses as well as animate the inbetweens and finalize the animation.

Cause and Effect

A story is a sequence of events. Each event has an effect on the next. Cause and effect, therefore, drive both the story and the way a character is animated.

The cause can be any sort of action, from a force of nature to the actions of another character. The effect is how your character deals with those actions. Your character smells smoke—he looks around for flames. Your character sees a bully walking down the street—he decides to turn in the other direction. Your character hears funky music—he starts dancing. In some cases, the causes are filtered through the senses: a character smells smoke, sees a bully, hears music, and then reacts.

In other situations, the cause of an action is internal, perhaps drawn from a memory. A character recalls a pleasant childhood moment and smiles. A starving character remembers the taste of apple pie and his mouth waters. In these cases, the eyes still matter. A character remembering something always moves its eyes as it searches for the memory.

The character smells smoke, and then reacts.

As a character searches its memory, the eyes follow along.

Object of Attention

As we move through the day, our attention shifts from place to place, from object to object. Things happen. Those things demand attention.

Right now, your attention is focused on this book. You're exercising only those parts of the body that are used for reading. The rest of your body is relaxed. If the telephone were suddenly to ring, your attention would shift away from this book to the telephone. You would then exercise those parts of the body needed to travel to the phone and pick up the receiver. You would forget about the book momentarily as you focused completely on the phone.

Lee Strasberg, the father of method acting, would say that, in this case, the individual's object of attention has changed from the book to the phone. The object of attention is a basic building block with which both actors and animators work. By having the character concentrate on the object representing the task at hand, the animator establishes a sense that the character is truly involved in what he is doing.

When a cat plays with a catnip toy in the kitchen, it uses only those muscles necessary to concentrate on the object of attention: the toy. The cat is simply trying to accomplish a specific "task": to conquer the toy. All other muscles are completely relaxed.

When the character is **reading a book**, he's exercising only those parts of the body that are used for reading. **When the phone rings**, the character's attention shifts completely to the phone. He momentarily forgets about the book.

If the dog dashes into the kitchen looking for a drink, the cat's body suddenly changes its demeanor as it focuses on the new object of attention: the dog. The cat may tense up and arch its back, but it still uses only those muscles necessary to concentrate on its new object of attention. The cat's task has changed and she has momentarily forgotten the toy; her new task is to put the dog in its place.

The dog's object of attention, which had been "water," now becomes "the cat," and his original objective to "drink water" now becomes "growl at the cat." The dog is using only those muscles necessary to accomplish this task. He is focused on the cat, not the water.

Clarity

Making your character 100 percent focused on the task at hand gives your performance clarity. The audience knows exactly what the character is thinking at any given moment. Even when a character is distracted momentarily, it focuses 100 percent of its attention on the distraction for that fleeting moment.

Take the dog and cat situation a step further. Perhaps the dog becomes indecisive. He really needs that drink but still has to deal with the pesky cat. If you split the difference, the dog focuses 50 percent of the way between the cat and the water. The audience then wonders, "Why is the dog staring into space?"

The dog really needs that cool drink…

…but it also needs to deal with the cat. Even when your character cannot make up its mind, it is fully focused on one possibility or the other.

Even in its indecision, the dog needs to switch between objects of attention: 100 percent on the water, 100 percent on the cat. He looks longingly at the water, then turns back to growl at the cat. When he is looking at the water, he can really imagine that cool drink. When he is facing the cat, he is totally absorbed in that task.

If your character is 100 percent focused in the scene, the performance is crystal clear. If the character is not focused, the performance is muddy. Even when your character cannot make up its mind, it is fully focused on one possibility or the other.

Simplicity

Another way to achieve clarity is through simplicity. An old animation adage is "one thing at a time." This is similar to the concept of attention, but it also helps clarify the individual actions. A character trips, then falls, then gets up—it doesn't do them all at once.

You also should be clear as to what the individual action represents. Don't animate anger—that's too broad and general. What is the focus of the anger? It's better to animate "I hate my boss." This simplifies the emotion as well as gives your character focus. To give the emotion more depth, add the survival objective "I am angry at my boss, but I need my job to survive." This adds even more depth to the emotion so that the audience can truly empathize with the character.

In addition, try to simplify each of your character's poses and actions to keep them as clear as possible. The actions are like the links of a chain. They all fit together sequentially. If each action is clear and easily read, that link of the chain is strong. An overly complex pose or action could possibly break the chain and lose the audience.

Keep your poses simple and direct.

The Moment Before

One aspect of a character that is often overlooked is what the character was doing just before the scene started. Imagine a character entering a locker room. Is the character coming in off the street? Coming back from a heavy workout? Returning from a losing game? Each of these situations affects how the character carries itself when it enters the scene. Knowing what happened in the moments before this moment helps you keep your character focused.

As the character walks in the door, he conveys to the audience what happened the moment before.

Character Status

When animating multiple characters in a scene, you need to determine their status in relation to one another. Understanding who is "top dog," so to speak, helps tremendously in guiding the interactions between your characters.

A servant always defers to the master. In politics, everyone is expected to stand when the President walks into the room. A drill sergeant dominates his recruits. These are all extreme examples, but status is important in any society, and it translates to every aspect of our dealings with others, no matter how subtle. One character is always more dominant, and others are more submissive.

Which character has the higher status?

There is also a status transaction that happens regardless of rank and file and has to do with who is commanding the scene at the time. If you handle your poses in a way that clearly illustrates who is in control of the scene, the emotions will be more easily read. An example would be a man proposing marriage to a woman. He is in control of the scene when proposing, and then she is in control with her response. One is not necessarily higher than the other in a sense of society or rank and file, but each has a command of the scene at different times.

Status is displayed through body posture. The character with the higher status usually stands tall and projects his energy outward with a steady gaze. A submissive character leans forward and gazes down, sending his energy toward the floor.

Another clue to status and/or dominance can be illustrated using a technique called "mirroring." The submissive character will copy or mirror the dominant character's actions. This should appear to be a subconscious action on the character's part and is very subtle.

Givens

Whenever you work with a character, certain things are "given" to you to work with. These are the things you cannot change about the character. You may or may not agree with some of the decisions made before you took control of the character, but you need to accept these givens and use them to your advantage.

Voice recordings are one of the biggest givens for the animator. Typically, this is positive, because a good voice performance is an excellent foundation from which to build convincing animation. Big conflicts can arise, however, when an animator doesn't agree with the voicing of the character.

Other givens include the design of the character, the virtual sets, and other constraints. If you are integrating a character with live action, you may have to go so far as to match your character's movements with that of a live-action actor.

With any of these givens, the trick is to use them to your advantage. Working with the director may help to clarify the choices that were made before the work got to you. The cleverest choices often arise from limitations.

Acting and the Body

Every animator should know how the body moves as it reacts to stimuli. In acting, as in modeling, the body can be broken up into a few major parts. The head and face are important, as are the hands. The spine and its position also factor into how a character is perceived.

The Head

The head is the center of the intellect. The position of the head determines, to a large extent, how the audience perceives a character. Cocking the head to the side throws the body off center. Generally, this can indicate confusion, but it can also denote curiosity. When a character affirms something, his head may nod slightly; when a character disagrees, his head may shake slightly from side to side.

When the head is held up, exposing the throat, it indicates a more naive and childlike character—kids are short and they look up a lot. When the head is down, hiding the neck, the character is more authoritative and serious. Think of Jerry Lewis. When he was young and paired with Dean Martin in the 1950s, his character was that of an innocent and naive man. He kept his head high. When Jerry Lewis hosted the telethon, he had to be a lot more compelling. In this instance, he lowered his head.

Cocking the head to one side can indicate curiosity. **Raised high**, the head is more childlike. **Lowering the head** indicates authority.

One simple animation trick used to convey the notion of thought is to use anticipation: Always lead with the eyes or the head. The eyes move first, focusing the character's attention several frames before the head moves. The head should move next, followed a few frames later by the body. The eyes let the audience see that a character is thinking.

The Shoulders

Shoulders often express mood or emotion. In some respects, their motions are related to those of the hands, but shoulders can express themselves outside of hand motions. The shrug is a good example of expression through shoulder motions. A character pushing its way through a crowd may lead with the shoulders, much as a linebacker does.

The general position of the shoulders can also indicate mood. Slumped shoulders indicate weariness, while squared shoulders indicate alertness. If a character is defending itself, it turns the body and raises the shoulder facing the attacker, because this presents a smaller target to the attacker than if the character were to face it directly.

Slumped shoulders can indicate weakness or weariness. **Squared shoulders** are more forceful. Shoulders can also indicate emotion, as in this **shrug**.

The Hands

The big question from most animators is what to do with the hands. Some hand positions are universal in their meaning. Hands folded across the chest, for example, indicate that a character is closing itself off. Hands clasped behind the back are an indication of respect and lower status. A character with one hand on the hip might appear relaxed, whereas both hands on the hips make a character appear to be confrontational.

Where the hands are raised in relation to the body can also communicate a great deal about the character's demeanor. If the character raises his hands above the shoulders, it is a more intellectual gesture. Anxiety is a very intellectual emotion, and anxious people tend to hold their hands fairly high. Hands held lower are more primitive. A construction worker gesturing at a pretty girl will position his hands below his chest.

The Spine

The spine is very important to the overall look of the body. The spinal cord is where all the sensory data from the body is transmitted to the brain. The spinal cord also has a bit of its own intelligence—many reflex actions actually happen in the spinal cord rather than the brain.

Hands above the head are more intellectual.

Hands held lower are more primitive.

Hands near the chest are more emotive.

Posture is a very important indicator of a character's nature and demeanor. Your mom always told you to stand up straight for a reason. A proud character stands tall and arches its back to stick the chest out. Conversely, a depressed character tends to hunch over more. As the body ages, the spine stiffens, which makes it difficult for older characters to twist the spine and turn around.

The spine also figures prominently in status negotiations between characters. A character with high status stands taller and straighter. This goes pretty much for any character with higher self-worth. Such a character tends to keep its weight at the center of its body, near the hips. Characters with lower status subconsciously lower themselves by bending their spines and lowering their shoulders.

The Body and Chakras

When you're trying to understand a character, you need to understand where on the body the character's personality emanates. One way to look at this is with a bit of Eastern philosophy and the concept of a chakra.

The word "chakra" is Sanskrit for "wheel" or "disk" and signifies one of seven basic energy centers in the body. Each of these centers correlates to major nerve ganglia branching from the spinal column. The chakras also correlate to levels of consciousness, developmental stages of life, colors, sounds, body functions, and much, much more.

For animators, the best way to understand this concept is that the more primitive the emotion, the lower it sits on the spine. This little tidbit can be used as a guide to animating a character. The character's personality emanates most strongly from that point on the body. Primitive personalities, such as Rocky Balboa's, emanate from low on the body. The personalities of people who love others tend to emanate from the heart, or the middle chakra. The personality of an intellectual character like Woody Allen emanates from the head.

In general, the three lower chakras correspond with the main needs, such as survival, fertility, and free will, whereas the four higher chakras are related to a character's psychological makeup and define love, communication, and knowledge, as well as spirituality.

The seven chakras affect different
areas of the body.

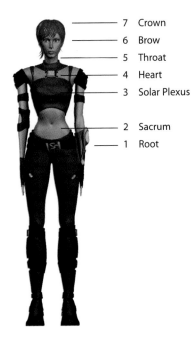

7	Crown
6	Brow
5	Throat
4	Heart
3	Solar Plexus
2	Sacrum
1	Root

The Seven Chakras and Personality

CHAKRA	ISSUES	GOALS	DESIRES	PERSONALITY
1. Root	Survival, grounding	Self-preservation	Stability, health, prosperity	Physical
2. Sacrum	Sexuality, emotions, desire	Self-gratification	Pleasure, sexuality, feeling	Emotional
3. Solar plexuss	Power, will	Self-definition	Spontaneity, purpose, self-esteem	Egoist
4. Heart	Love, relationships	Self-acceptance	Compassion, acceptance, relationships	Social
5. Throat	Communication	Self-expression	Communication, creativity, resonance	Creative
6. Brow	Intuition, imagination	Self-reflection	Perception, interpretation, imagination	Perceptive
7. Crown	Awareness	Self-knowledge	Wisdom, knowledge, consciousness	Intellectual

Other Techniques

There are dozens of other acting techniques and theories about acting. Basically, they all boil down to psychology and how to get the body to do things it would not normally do. How many people can actually cry on cue? Not many, I imagine. An actor with sufficient training, however, can do such a task reliably. As an animator, you never need to cry on cue, but understanding some of these techniques can help you empathize with your character and animate it better.

Sense Memory

If you have ever been really hungry, the thought of food was probably enough to actually make your mouth water. This is an example of your senses remembering the taste of the food and your body responding accordingly by activating your salivary glands. As an animator, you can use your sense memory to conjure up emotions and actions for your character.

If your character is hungry, try to remember the last time you were truly hungry. How did it feel? Did it make you light-headed? How did you move? Slowly? Were you easily agitated? When an animator does a sensory exercise, he may find emotional responses occurring that he may not have anticipated.

Animal Exercises

If you are having problems trying to understand a character, you may need to look at it from a different angle. One method is to try re-creating the character as an animal. What animal does your character move and act like?

When doing this exercise, you need to be very specific in your observation. Go to the zoo and watch the animal for at least an hour. What is the animal's posture? How does it move? When does it move? Why does it move? Can you imagine what the animal might be thinking?

If you can, try to physically imitate the animal's motions. Again, be as specific as possible. Look into the animal's eyes. Does it seem intelligent? Tame? Wild? Dangerous? Try to transfer the animal's thoughts to your own thoughts.

Of course, in animation, you often have to animate animals themselves. Many times, this demands the same sorts of observations. In some cases, however, the animals don't act like the bodies they inhabit. Think of the elephant Shep in the live-action remake of *George of the Jungle*. The elephant was raised as a pet, and acted more like a dog than an elephant, even going as far as to fetch a "stick," which was actually a 6-foot log. In this case, a couple of hours spent watching your dog would be very helpful.

Affective Memory

The use of affective memory is one of the most widely known procedures in all of "method" acting. Simply put, it tries to put an actor as close to a character as possible by asking him to recall a similar event or experience in his own life.

This technique is used most notably in the sorts of scenes that expect an actor to dig really deep. These are scenes with a very strong emotional content, such as when a character loses his best friend to murder, a character's spouse demands a divorce, or a character discovers he has an incurable disease. In these situations it may be necessary for the animator to find similar experiences in his own life and to be first willing and then able to relive those experiences as the character is animated.

This technique is most often mentioned when characters are in stressful and traumatic situations. But affective memory can also be used for lighter moments as well. If your character wins the lottery, try to recall a moment in your life when you had a similar experience that both shocked you and made you joyously happy.

Conclusion

Understanding the art of acting is very important to any character animator. Actors use an arsenal of techniques to inhabit their characters, and animators can use these same techniques to better animate their characters. Study your characters and understand their personalities and motivations. Use this knowledge to let the character tell you how it needs to be posed and moved. Naturalness and spontaneity come from inside the character, and acting skills will help you get there.

CHAPTER TEN

Directing and Filmmaking

In its most basic form, directing character animation is about telling a story. Characters drive the story, and the story, in turn, further defines the character. A good story gives characters motivation, conflict, and a path of action. Without these things, your characters will not truly spring to life.

Knowing how to tell a good story will help your animation skills immensely. If you understand where a story is in any particular scene, you will have a good idea of how each of the characters needs to act and behave to further the story. For those interested in making their own films, having a good story is the first thing any filmmaker needs.

On top of good storytelling skills, directing requires knowledge of the entire filmmaking process. Directors need to be able to work with everyone, from the client to the voice actors to the animators and all the people in between. The best way to learn these skills is to make your own film and tell your own stories.

   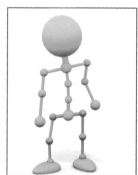

Characters and Story

The first step in creating animation is deciding what it will be about—in other words, the story. You will also need to decide what characters will be involved in this story. Do you develop the story or the characters first?

You may already have a story you want to tell. In that case, you'll need to develop the characters to tell the story. On the other hand, you may have a library of characters you have modeled and want to use. In this case, you'll need to develop a story for the characters you're familiar with. Television series, for example, are written this way; the characters remain relatively constant and the stories are tailored to them.

The character determines how the role will play. Should you cast this character as a hero or villain?

Wherever you decide to start, you will soon realize that story and character are very tightly coupled. The story you choose will help define the characters through their actions. Strong characters will, in turn, affect the story. Sir Lawrence Olivier as Hamlet plays much differently than Mel Gibson in the same role. Imagining a character such as Bugs Bunny in that role brings forth even more hilarious differences.

For a character to come to life, it will need motivation to make it want to do something and obstacles to make that task more interesting by causing conflict. These ingredients also make a good story.

Motivation Creates Character

In order for a character to do anything within a story, the character must be motivated. Characters are motivated by their needs: A little tramp is hungry and needs food. A powerful newspaper magnate needs money and power. Laurel and Hardy need to deliver a piano. What a character wants and needs determines who he or she is to the audience.

The way characters pursue their needs gives the audience clues to their personalities. Perhaps two characters are running for the same political office. One pursues it honestly; the other one uses every trick in the book. They both need the same thing—political office—but their personalities cause them to go about it differently. Another good example might be the simple task of jumping over a puddle. Fred Astaire would do it gracefully, while Buster Keaton might trip and land flat on his face.

Obstacles Create Conflict

If you can identify what your characters need, you can also create obstacles for them to overcome. This is what adds interest to the story. If Laurel and Hardy deliver the piano without incident, the story falls flat. Place a very steep staircase in their way, and they have an obstacle to overcome. The comedy is derived from the many ways the piano can slip from their hands and fall down the stairs. Overcoming the obstacle of the stairs is what creates the comedy. Obstacles can be physical, such as a staircase, but they can also take other forms. A character may need to overcome fear, for example. In any case, obstacles are the things that create conflict in a story.

This character is hungry, and the desire for food is a motivation.

This character is late for a wedding. The obstacles create conflict.

Conflict Creates Drama

Stories are about conflict. A character simply walking down the street is not a story. It is also not very interesting. The character needs motivation—perhaps he is late and desperately needs to get to his wedding. If the street is littered with banana peels, you have an obstacle, which creates conflict and the beginnings of a story. Does the character avoid the peels? Does the character slip? If so, when? Does he make it to the wedding, and in what shape? It is up to the storyteller to make the most of the situation.

Of course, larger conflicts can generate much more intricate and substantial stories. Complexity adds spice to a story. Still, you need to be sure your story line is clear and not overly burdened by excessive complexity. There should typically be one main motivation and conflict in the story, with a limited number of secondary conflicts to add interest.

For example, consider a simple story: A bumbling scientist creates a monster that escapes the lab and terrorizes the city. Unfortunately, he can't bear to kill his creation. This simple story has several conflicts. The main conflict is the scientist trying to overcome the love he feels for his creation, but secondary conflicts are many: finding a way to destroy the monster, not getting killed by the monster, and so on.

Another example might be a wrongfully accused man who escapes from prison and must avoid the police while trying to clear his name. The conflict of keeping away from the cops is obvious, but the man's true motivation is proving his innocence. This is what drives the story. The cops and the chase simply add more obstacles and conflict to keep the story interesting.

The way a character handles conflict tells the audience something about his personality. If the mad scientist can't kill his creation, it's because he has feelings of love for the creature. This, in turn, will evoke empathy from the audience.

Conflict can also be much subtler. Many stories deal with internal conflicts, such as a character struggling with personal demons, growing up, or changing in some way. Internal conflict, however, will most likely manifest itself externally. An insecure character, for example, may act subordinate to a domineering spouse. The conflict is resolved only when the character confronts the insecurity and stands up to the spouse. In this case, the spouse represents the inner conflict. The events leading up to the confrontation are what tell the story.

Stories are a circular thing. Characters are driven by motivations, and blocking the way are obstacles, which cause conflict, which further defines the characters.

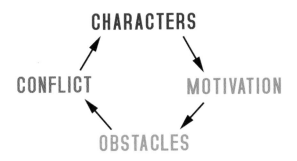

Just as in war, when a conflict ends, there is resolution. This is the "payoff" of the story. In the case of the fugitive, the real perpetrator is caught and our hero goes free. Or he doesn't. Too often, resolutions take the form of "and they lived happily ever after." This might be nice for a children's story, but resolutions work best when the ending has a slight twist—one last surprise for the audience.

Visual Storytelling

When writing a novel, an author can delve into the mind of a character to tell you what he or she is thinking. A line such as "Mary was happy with herself" could very easily be written into a novel with no problems at all. In a script, however, these sorts of statements can cause tremendous problems. We can't just say Mary is happy, we have to show it—how else will the audience know what she is feeling? They're not reading a script, they're watching a film. Mary will need to demonstrate her change of emotion through an action that the audience can see.

If this character says "I'm so happy," the audience will think he is happy.

How she demonstrates this emotion will also give the audience clues to her character. If she is a shy person, perhaps she will simply smile. A more gregarious Mary might jump for joy. Perhaps the moment could include dialogue in addition to the action. However, her actions are what define Mary to the audience.

Film and animation are primarily visual media, and studies have shown that visuals are more important than audio: if the audio contradicts the image, the image will win. Politicians have been known to use this fact with great results. If a politician is seen on the news in a visually appealing or patriotic setting, viewers will think more positively about the politician, even if the news reporter's audio narration says negative things.

If this character says "I'm so happy," the meaning is unclear and the visual wins over the dialogue.

This is not to say that dialogue and audio are unimportant. Sound effects are very important. What a character says is extremely important. What the character does, however, is always most important. The image defines the sound, not the other way around. A line of dialogue like "I'm so happy" will read straight if the character is smiling and acting happy. If the character acts sad as he says this, the image will win, and the audience will interpret the character as sad, ironic, or both. When writing a script for animation, you must take the visuals into account at all points.

Developing a Story

The essence of story structure is simple. You'll start with a character who is motivated by a need. To meet that need, the character must overcome obstacles. As the character deals with the obstacles, the audience learns more about who the character is. The concept is simple to explain, but telling a story well is an art form. Now that you understand some of the basic elements of storytelling, you can start to develop stories of your own.

What type of story will you create? There are quite a few. There's the simple story with a full plot that has a beginning, middle, and end. There are also stories that are really just a collection of gags strung together, as in a Road Runner cartoon. Even those simple cartoons have the essential basics of a story—the Coyote's motivation is to catch the Road Runner. He just seems to encounter plenty of obstacles along the way.

Keep It Simple

While it is wonderful to imagine the most incredible and complex stories, there will always be limits. Even the biggest studio blockbuster has a fixed budget, and for a one-person production, the limit is the amount of time that you can give to the project. Most projects fall somewhere in the middle of these extremes.

With any project, there is always the tendency to bite off more than you can chew. Creating a story is easy. Actually producing it is another matter altogether. It is always best to keep your time and budget constraints in mind. Knowing how much time and effort will be required to produce a particular film is knowledge gained mostly from experience—the more films you make, the more aware you will be of the time and expense involved.

If you are a student creating your first film, the best advice is to keep it small. This means sticking to a handful of characters and a situation that is manageable. Usually two to three minutes is plenty, and four to five minutes is ambitious. Films longer than five minutes might require some outside help. Remember, the classic Warner Brothers cartoons were all only six minutes long.

Simplicity is typically the best way to go. Most of the best short films have very simple plots and stories. The Pixar shorts are great examples: they each have only a handful of characters and one simple conflict. Another case for keeping the story simple and the number of characters small is that you can spend more screen time developing each character, and isn't "character" what character animation is all about?

Brainstorming a Premise

There are many ways to develop stories. One way is simply to brainstorm ideas. Brainstorming is an exercise in pure creativity. If you prefer to write out your thoughts, get a sheet of paper and start writing down ideas. If you like to work the story out visually, you can also make simple sketches.

Your story should have at least one character, one motivation, and one obstacle. It could be as simple as a child trying to open a childproof container. Or you could turn that idea on its head and have the adult be incapable of opening the container, while the child, the dog, and even the pet hamster have it all figured out. A character could be extremely hungry, but food is hard to get. You could base your story on a traditional fairy tale—maybe the three little pigs who build houses out of straw, twigs, and bricks to avoid the wolf. If you want to add a twist to that concept, make them the three little lab rats who build mazes out of DNA to avoid the scientist. As you can see, the core idea of a film can be stated very simply in one or two lines. This simple statement is called a *premise*. Creating a good premise is your first step in creating a good film.

Developing Your Premise into a Story

As you can see, the possibilities for premises are limited only by your imagination. Once you have a premise in hand, you need to ask yourself some very serious and objective questions about how the film will be made.

The first question is whether the film can be made at all. If it's a story about fish, for instance, you may need to animate water. If your story is about a barber, you may need to animate realistic hair. Ask yourself if your software is capable of handling the types of shots and characters the premise demands. If not, you may want to choose another premise or put the premise into another setting.

You also need to think about length. Some stories cannot be told in a few minutes, though you'd be surprised at how much you can cram into that span of time. Many commercials tell great little stories in 30 to 60 seconds. Simple is usually better, however. Typically, this means focusing on one set of characters, one motivation, and one set of conflicts.

One way to flesh out your story is by going through another brainstorming session to generate as many ideas related to the story as possible. Write these ideas down on note cards, so you can keep track of them and arrange them into a story.

If your premise is good, you can generate plenty of ideas—far too many to fit within your time constraints. Should you have too much material, you can think of it as either a luxury or a curse: If deleting the extra material from your story makes it incomprehensible, your story might be cursed with too much complexity. You probably need to take a step backward to rethink the premise or the major story points to get the film to a manageable length. If you can toss out material and still have a sound story, then you have the luxury of too much good stuff. Keeping only the best material will make your film that much stronger. Even if you have lots of great material, don't delude yourself into thinking that it all needs to be put in the film. Every extra bit of material means an extra animation for you to complete. If you bite off more than you can chew, it can come back to haunt you later.

Developing a Script

Once you have a ton of ideas, you'll have a stack of note cards and will need to organize your story so that you know, beat for beat, the exact sequence of events, including the ending. Let's take the idea of the adult who can't open the childproof bottle. Getting to the contents of the bottle is the adult's motivation; the complex cap is the obstacle. Pretty simple story.

In fleshing the story out, you could have the adult use all sorts of wild schemes to get the cap off: a can opener, a blowtorch, dynamite. If other characters, like a kid, a dog, and a hamster, manage to open the bottle with no help, it can just serve to humiliate the adult and strengthen his motivation, as he sees that his goal is possible.

Organizing the story means that you need to build the gags, one at a time. A simple structure might be alternating the adult's attempts with those of the other characters. The adult tries opening the bottle by hand, gives up, and then the child comes in and opens it. This motivates the adult further, who resorts to more drastic measures. These fail, and then another character opens the bottle. The adult's battle with the bottle escalates further, and so on.

All of these conflicts need to build to an ending as well. The ending could be simple, with the adult driving himself crazy with frustration. It could be ironic: he finally opens the bottle, only to find it empty. It could be a bit more fantastic: he has such a pounding headache that his head explodes. Or you could make a surreal *Twilight Zone* ending, where the adult and his world are itself contained within another giant childproof bottle. Again, there are an infinite number of twists and possibilities to any story.

As you finalize the structure of your story, you will also need to be writing a script. This could be as simple as a point-by-point outline of the action or as extensive as a full script, with dialogue and screen direction. Scripts do not have to be written documents; some directors dispense with written scripts and go straight to storyboard so they can visualize their film as it is written.

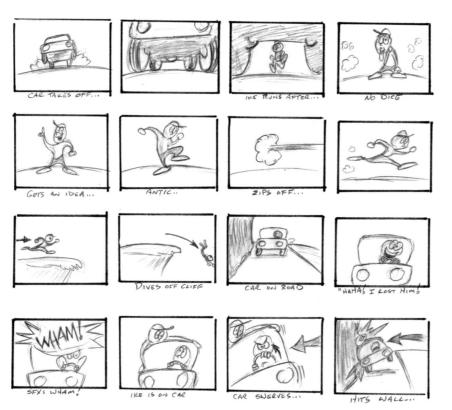

A good storyboard can replace a written script.

Adding Dialogue

As you write the script, you may also find it necessary to add dialogue. This is certainly not a requirement, as many of the best cartoons have no dialogue whatsoever. Dialogue does help considerably in defining your characters, however. A good script and voice performance will help your characters appear real and will make their personalities pop off the screen. A good voice track is also great for animators, who can use it to guide the performance.

If you decide to add dialogue to your film, you will need to hone your writing skills. Writing dialogue that sounds natural and unforced can be difficult. A couple of handy hints might make the process easier. First, listen to real conversations, perhaps even putting them on tape and transcribing them to see how they work. You'll notice that people tend to speak in short sentences or fragments, interrupting each other in many cases. Another way to get a sense of dialogue is to imagine a character as a famous personality. If he's a tough guy, for example, does he talk like Robert DeNiro, Humphrey Bogart, or Marlon Brando? Using a famous character's speech patterns as a guide is a good way to get started with the writing process. Hopefully, the character will take on a life of his or her own and diverge from the guide. If you base your character on a famous personality, however, you will need to be careful with voice casting—don't have your actors imitate the voice as well. (Unless, of course, you're doing a parody.)

One problem that happens time and time again is too much dialogue. Long stretches of dialogue can eat up valuable screen time. Unless the dialogue is extremely well directed and acted, it can also drag down the quality of a film. While this is not a hard-and-fast rule, most animation benefits from short, snappy dialogue. A sentence or two per character is usually all that is needed to cover the action and keep the film moving along. Short bits of dialogue are also easier to direct and animate. If a character needs to speak paragraphs, it had better be for a very good reason. One rule of thumb in live action is that the audience's attention span is only about 20 seconds. Try listening to any speech that goes on for more than that without drifting. Since animation usually moves along faster than live action, the attention span is even shorter.

Visualizing Your Story

At this point, in addition to writing the script, you'll need to be visualizing how the film will look. Animation is a very visual medium, so you will absolutely need to see how your film looks in every shot. Even if you draw in stick figures, sketching out your ideas in storyboard form will help you understand exactly how the gags and situations in your film will be staged.

The key here is to block out the film, not make pretty pictures. Accuracy in the look of the characters is less important at this stage than the composition and flow of the film as a whole. As long as the storyboard conveys the idea, it doesn't matter what it looks like—especially if it's only for your own use. It is also easy to fall in love with the drawing of a bad shot because of the time investment. If a client needs to see "clean" boards, do them after you've worked out the details.

As you create the boards, take the opportunity to look for holes in the story, or possible gags. You may find that certain gags that sounded great in your script don't work visually, and it is much better, and cheaper, to make that cut now, rather than when the film is complete.

While sketching storyboard panels can be very quick for some people, others have problems with drawing. Drawing 3D characters by hand might be less accurate, as the drawings might not be true to the actual characters. If your characters are already built, you can visualize the story in another way, without drawing. Simply pose the characters in your 3D application, and render stills to use as the storyboard. No scanning is required, the images are true to the actual characters, and the 3D scene files can be saved and used later as layouts for animation.

Producing a Film

Once you have your story written and storyboarded, it's time to actually produce the film. Making an animated film can be a solitary endeavor, or it can be a group effort. Regardless of the size of the team, however, it is not an easy task. You need to be organized and dedicated to completing the film. Whether you're making a student film or a feature, the steps required are pretty much the same.

Developing a Budget

All films have a budget of some sort. In a commercial film, this budget would involve time and money. For a personal film, it could just be a free summer, a computer, and a heck of a lot of time. In either event, you need to develop a rough budget. With any project, there are three conflicting goals:

- Make the best-quality film.

- Make it at the lowest possible price.

- Make it as quickly as possible.

When confronted with these choices, you'll usually need to pick two. The trick is to balance all three so you get a film that works but also comes in on time and within budget. Doing so may require clever design, scheduling, and budgeting—or freebies from a friend at the post house. However you get it done, try to make quality your number-one goal, because when people see a film they judge it by its quality, not by how much it cost or how quickly it was produced.

Sadly, nobody has infinite resources, and all animated films have a budget. Animation is a very creative pursuit, and placing time and limits on the creative process is never easy. That's why they invented things like producers to do the dirty work of creating a budget. Remember, a budget can be monetary, but it can also take other forms; you'll need to consider deadlines and air dates, as well as the number of people available to work on the project.

A budget is simply a fixed amount of time, money, or quality, and it can be good for your work. If you have an infinite amount of time to get something done, chances are good that it will never get done. Limits force you to make decisions, invent novel solutions, and, most importantly, get the project finished.

Story and Budget

Writers can very easily create stories that are rich, complex, and detailed; all they have to do is write more words. Ink is cheap. Film is expensive, and in film, some ideas simply cost more to produce than others. In live action, a simple film with a handful of characters is a lot cheaper to produce than a big action blockbuster. The same goes for animation. The more charac-ters, sets, and props a movie uses, the more time and money each minute of screen time is going to require.

Think about movies you have seen recently and how many different loca-tions they had to use. Typically, the more locations there are, the more expensive the film. Animation is very similar. More locations mean more sets and more expense. Even the choice of shots affects the budget: a long shot chosen over a close shot can make a difference because you have to build more for the long shot.

Many writers and story people hate to be told that an idea is just too expen-sive to produce. But if you try to produce something that's too expensive for the given budget, then corners must invariably be cut and the project is bound to suffer in terms of quality. It is much better to work from ideas that are achievable from the start.

Design and Budget

One way to address a budget is to design characters and props that meet the budget. If you design highly realistic characters, the audience will expect highly realistic animation. If you don't have the budget for this, quality will suffer. If your budgets are tight, it makes much more sense to design simpler characters. That way, the audience's expectations will not be so high.

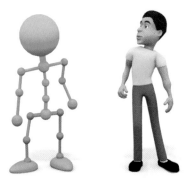

Design affects budget. The simple character will be cheaper to animate than the more complex character.

Reuse and Budgeting

One way to lower budgets is to reuse characters, props, and backgrounds. This may not be possible for a single film, but it is very important for such things as a television series. Once a character is built, it can be used over and over. The only additional investment is animation time. The same goes for sets and props. Many series limit the number of sets, forcing writers to make do with the inventory at hand.

Setting Deadlines

Time, or rather the lack of it, is always a factor when making a film. Part of any budget is the time allotted to complete the project. Most commercial projects have very strict deadlines, and even student films are due at the end of the semester. The only project that might have no deadline is the personal film. Without a deadline, however, many personal films tend to sit around for years before they get finished. It's best to think of a deadline as the finish line of a race—finishing the race gives you a sense of accomplishment.

A good budget has reasonable deadlines. As is often the case when money is involved, however, many budgets tend to cut corners. Shaving a week or a month off the schedule may save a production money, but it is also sure to dig into the quality of the finished project.

Deciding exactly how much time to budget for a project requires years of experience. Most novices (and many experts, for that matter) tend to underestimate the amount of time required. It almost always takes longer than you think. If in doubt, always add a fudge factor—double or triple your original estimate.

You can use many rules of thumb when budgeting a project. One may be the number of seconds an animator can produce in a week. Of course, this number will vary depending on the project. An animator on a feature film may produce only 3 to 10 seconds per week, but it is very high-quality animation. Games are another story: for the short cinematic sequences in games, 3 to 10 seconds a day, and for gameplay, at least 3 moves a day are reasonable goals. An animator on an animated TV series, on the other hand, may have to produce as much as 20 to 60 seconds per week, but at a lower quality. As you can see, these numbers vary widely depending on the material.

In addition to animator time, dozens of other factors need to be considered. How much time is needed to write the script? Record the dialogue? Create the storyboards? Get approval from the network? Other factors may be technical, such as how much time it takes to render the project. If it takes three days to render all the frames and the project is due tomorrow, you're dead meat. All these factors, plus many others, must be worked into a coherent schedule.

Developing a Schedule

You'll need to consider many factors in creating a schedule. The best way to look at these factors is to put everything into a grid of some sort. Many producers use scheduling programs or custom spreadsheets to work it all out. Putting together a good schedule is a lot like putting together an assembly line: after one part of the process is complete, the next department picks up the work and adds to it. For example, you can't animate a character until it is built, so modeling, rigging, and layout must happen before animation.

Some tasks can overlap. In a feature film environment, many studios develop and model the characters concurrently with the script and storyboard creation. This allows the animators to start work much sooner after the storyboard is locked. Rendering is another task that can be overlapped. After a shot is finished, it can be rendered while the other shots are animated.

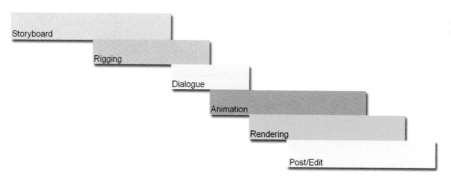

Storyboard

Rigging

Dialogue

Animation

Rendering

Post/Edit

A simple schedule overlaps tasks for efficiency.

The best schedule interleaves all of the required tasks seamlessly, so that the film is completed cleanly and efficiently, with no waiting around. Of course, all sorts of issues that threaten to undermine the schedule are sure to pop up during production, but with a well-planned schedule, these can be accounted for much more easily. It's also good to add in a bit of a cushion for those times when everything goes wrong. If the project is due in 10 weeks, you might create an 8-week schedule just to be sure that when tasks slip, you'll still hit the final deadline.

Assembling a Crew

Animation is a lot of work, and most films require a crew of people. For small projects, this crew can be a handful of people; for feature films, the crew can number in the hundreds.

Regardless of the number of actual people involved, there are quite a few job descriptions associated with filmmaking, and you'll need to be familiar with each of them. If you're working alone, you may find that you'll be doing most or all of these jobs yourself. If, however, you're working as part of a larger team, you may be doing only one of these jobs—or in the case of a smaller production, you may find that you're managing a handful of tasks. Regardless of where you find yourself, the following list should be helpful.

Producers. These come in a number of flavors. At the top of the heap is the executive producer, who does the business development and funds the project. Executive producers typically deal with clients. A bit lower on the totem pole may be a supervising producer who manages the day-to-day tasks and may delegate responsibility to even more producers. These may include line producers, creative producers, animation producers, and perhaps a few others. Generally, all producers are involved in managing the production in one way or another.

Director. The main creative force on the project. The director supervises just about everything, including story, dialogue recording, modeling, animation, and postproduction. Some studios break up the directing job: they may have a voice director who does nothing but direct the voice talent, an animation director, an art director, a creative director, and so on.

Writer/storyboard artist. The people who create and visualize the story. Writers tend to work with words; storyboard artists tend to work with pictures. Both have the same goal: coming up with a clever and coherent story.

Voice talent. The voices of the characters. A good voice actor has a very nimble and versatile voice and excellent acting skills.

Modeling. A sculptor, essentially, who works on a computer and creates all the characters and props. Some modelers have been known to dabble in clay and may scan in their physical sculptures. A good modeler knows how to build characters that animate well.

Textures/lighting. A painter who works on the computer. The texture artist is responsible for creating textures and writing shaders that are applied to the characters and props. The texture person may also manage lighting.

Technical director. An artist with a strong technical bent. Technical directors know a lot about the software and can usually do some programming. They do all sorts of tasks, from rigging characters to laying out scenes, doing camera work, writing shaders, and managing renders to writing custom software and plug-ins.

Animator. The person who brings the characters to life. A good animator has an excellent sense of acting and timing, as well as a strong knowledge of anatomy and motion.

Systems and support. The people who keep the computers running. This team can also include people dubbed "render wranglers," who manage rendering and final output on large projects, making sure each and every frame finds its way through the system.

Audio. People who record dialogue, as well as edit and mix the final soundtrack.

Composer. If there is original music, someone has to write it, and that's the composer. A good composer writes music that sets a mood but doesn't overpower the film.

Administrative. Of course, there are plenty of spots for administrative people such a production assistants, payroll, and so on.

It's always important to get good people for your projects—people who are not just talented artists, but who show up on time and hit the deadline with time to spare. Additionally, everyone has to get along; people with a professional work ethic make things go much more smoothly.

Of course, the best people are always busy (and usually expensive), so you may have to make some trade-offs when looking for people. In the case of a student film, you may have very little money to offer, but you can do trades and offer to help out on other students' projects in return for help on your film.

Developing the Story

As we have seen, the first task in making an animated film is developing the story. Most of the time, you pitch and sell the idea to get the money and time to create the film. Once you have the idea sold, a development and refinement process probably takes place before the film actually gets made. This means refining the raw idea into a film that can actually be made. Many productions spend almost as much time developing the story as they do in actual production.

In some cases, the story development and animation processes run concurrently. The main characters can be designed before the storyboard is complete, and modeling can also begin before the story is locked.

Designing the Production

As the story develops, the look of the characters and of the production should also develop. Sometimes this is a back-and-forth process in which the design decisions affect the story and vice versa. As the design is solidified, the modeling and texturing artists can start creating the assets for the production.

Design is one of the most critical tasks of a film. If an animation looks cool or interesting, your audience will notice it, and great design not only appeals to your audience, but also inspires the artists on your crew. (I know of a lot of productions that got extra attention from the crew just because the designs looked so cool.) Conversely, a bad design makes the production into "just another job" for the crew.

Modeling and Rigging

Character building and rigging must happen early in the production. You are likely to know who the major characters are even before the story is finalized—in many productions, the characters are built while the script is being written. In fact, you may need to create rough models of the characters to sell the project in the first place.

As the script and storyboard are finalized, you will have a much clearer idea of the modeling requirements. This enables you to model the secondary characters and props as the dialogue is recorded and the Leica reel is cut.

Recording Dialogue

Once the script and storyboard are finished, it's time to record dialogue—but before you do this, you need to cast your characters.

Casting your voice talent is one of the most critical tasks you face in making a film. If you can get excellent voice talent who give great performances, you will have great raw material for animators to use in creating an inspired acting performance.

The voice determines, to a large degree, how the audience perceives a character, and you should make every attempt to get it right. You may have to audition a number of actors in order to find the right voice.

Casting Voices

Selecting voices for a film is like assembling players for a band. The individual voices must complement one another, yet they must also all work together toward a common goal. Try to come up with a good mix of voices and textures. If two voices sound similar, it can get very confusing for the audience.

Casting is difficult for the director, but it can be even more stressful for actors. Most of them will be rejected, and only a few will get jobs. Respect this when holding a casting session. With actors who don't make the cut, be nice and be sure to pass along a compliment or two as you let them down.

What does this character sound like? Casting a low voice will make him scary; casting a high voice might make him funny.

You should always go into a casting session with an open mind. Often, you won't know the voice until you hear it. If you have a preconceived notion of how you want your character to sound, it biases you against what could be a better solution. Actors are creative people, and they can bring a lot to the process. Give them a bit of rope and let them try to "discover" the voice. After they nail it, let your directing skills kick in and fine-tune the performance.

When auditioning, listen to just the actor's voice, because that's all the audience will hear. It doesn't matter what the actor looks like; the sound is all that matters. A number of women perform voices for young boy characters, for example, but obviously could never play them on screen. You're not casting the person, just the person's voice. Many directors look away from the person who is auditioning so that the actor's gestures or appearance don't bias them.

If your budget is minimal, as in a personal film, you may have to rely on friends or even perform the voices yourself. This doesn't have to be a problem; you can get good performances from nonprofessionals. Aardman Animation has done some excellent films, such as *Creature Comforts*, among others, that use interviews with ordinary people as the dialogue track. People always sound more relaxed and natural when they're not trying to act and when they're talking about something personal.

Recording Dialogue

After you cast the actors, you can book a voice session to record your tracks. This is one of the most critical parts of the production process, because a lousy voice track cannot be saved with great animation. Typically, a voice session is also one of the most fun parts of the process. You hear the lines for the first time, which is exciting, and you also hear the jokes for the first time, which can be hilarious.

In a professional environment, the actors sit together in a booth, and a recording engineer operates the equipment. The director conducts the process, while various other people (producers, clients, etc.) usually gather and offer their sage advice—which the director may or may not take.

In a budget environment, try to get a decent recording in whatever way possible. This usually means getting good microphones and a quiet room. If you can, get a separate microphone for each actor.

Dialogue can be recorded one line at a time, or many lines can be recorded together, as in a radio play. You'll often have actors voice multiple characters, and in this case, you need to record lines individually. Recording lines one at a time makes editing much easier and allows you to easily introduce your own timing in the final material.

If your dialogue is quick, with characters stepping on each other's lines, you may need to record many lines in a single take. This can become tricky later, because it's much harder to edit this type of dialogue.

Directing Dialogue

The director needs to get the most out of each actor. This means communicating with the actors and letting them know what you expect. Before you record a scene, discuss it with the actors so they have an idea of how you see the action taking place. You also need to keep the actors fresh and spontaneous, so try to communicate your ideas quickly and concisely.

When recording, it's a good idea to get the actors into a creative flow, so they stay in character. Be sure to get stands for the scripts, so the actors can keep their hands free. Too many interruptions cause them to slip out of character, which prolongs the process and makes the acting stale. Try to keep things moving along when everyone is in character. The first few reads of a script are usually the best.

Most directors like to do multiple takes so that they have a variety of material to choose from. The best way to do this and still keep the actors fresh is to have the actors record the same line (or lines) three times in a row, usually known as A, B, and C takes (which can also stretch into many more if needed). By saying the lines multiple times, actors can vary the reads each time and stay within character. As you record, mark down the take you like. If you're not sure, ask the engineer for a playback.

If an actor is not reading a line the way you want, the first temptation is to just read the line yourself to give the actor a hint. This is not a good idea, because actors need to find the lines themselves. If they simply parrot the director, the line is certain to fall flat. Try to get your point across in different ways by telling the actor the line needs to be louder, softer, subtler, angrier, nicer, more condescending, etc. If you can't get the reading you want, you may need to come back to it at the end of the session, so the actor has a fresh take.

Ad-Lib

Some of the best voice actors are also very good comedians and improvisational actors. During the recording process, they may diverge from the script and throw in a few ad-lib lines. These can add a lot of spice and spontaneity to your film. On some productions, we've known our actors well enough to know that we can leave parts of the script open and allow them to fill in the blanks. You may also find that lines that looked great on paper don't sound as great when read. In this case, you may need to do a quick rewrite of the script in the recording studio or ask the actors to improvise something better.

Ad-libs and script changes, however, can be a real problem with clients and network executives. Most of these people have approval over the script, so any deviation from the script may need to go through another approval process. Be sure to record the original lines as well as the ad-libs so that you have a backup if the changes are rejected.

Cutting a Leica Reel

Once you have your storyboard and your dialogue, it's a good idea to cut a *Leica reel*, also known as an *animatic*. The Leica reel contains still images timed to the dialogue and music. The finished Leica reel looks like a slide show that plays like a rough version of your film. It tells you the length of each individual shot and locks down the timing of dialogue.

A video editing package like Avid, Final Cut, or Adobe Premiere is a good choice for creating Leica reels. The procedure is relatively straightforward, and the principles apply to other editing packages as well.

First, you should get digital versions of your storyboard panels. If you created them in 3D, the files already exist. If the storyboard is hand-drawn, the drawings need to be scanned. (For large storyboards, a scanner with a sheet feeder helps considerably.) If you have dialogue, you also need to import the audio into your computer. After you have these on your disk, you need to import all the storyboard picture files into your video editor.

Now it's simply a matter of clicking and dragging the individual pictures to the video timeline and adjusting their lengths so that the film plays the way you want. By dragging the edges of the image on the timeline, you can add time to or subtract time from each panel. If you have dialogue, it should be dragged to the timeline as well. Dialogue, however, is a fixed length—the only way to make it shorter is to cut words or sentences. As you work through the dialogue, you are also selecting the final takes from the recording session. You may need to jot down the exact takes for later so the audio engineer can match the tracks from the master tape.

After you've worked your way through all the dialogue and storyboard panels, render your Leica reel and watch it. If you need to, go back and make timing changes. You may also want to cut extraneous shots to tighten up the film, or add needed shots at this point. The finished Leica reel gives you a good idea of exactly how long your film will be, as well as exactly how long each shot in the film will be.

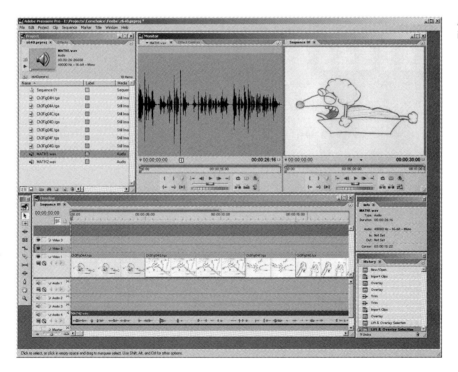

A Leica reel can be created in a nonlinear video editor.

Creating the Layout

After you've finished your Leica reel, the timing and shot selection for the film are also locked down. It's finally time to start animation production in earnest. The production team is likely to be building and rigging the primary characters and props long before the Leica reel is complete, though some productions hold off on secondary modeling because scenes can get cut during the animatic process. It makes no sense to build props for scenes that will never be animated.

Before the animators can begin animating, they need to have scene files that contain all the elements associated with the scene. These include any characters, props, backgrounds, and audio, among other things. This task is typically called *layout*. Technical directors usually perform the task, but animators have also been known to help lay out shots for animation.

Each layout varies depending on the requirements of the scene. If the animation involves a live-action composite, it may be as simple as placing the character in the shot and loading up the background plate. In a more complex shot, the artist doing layout may need to light the scene, rig characters, place props, and so on. The final layout should be a scene file that is ready to be animated.

Animating the Film

After the scenes have been laid out, you're finally ready to actually animate your film. That's what most of this book has been about, and animation is one of the truly fun parts of making a film.

When animating your film, the temptation is to animate every shot in sequential order, from beginning to end. This, however, is usually not the best way to proceed. The beginning of the film is very important to the rest of the film, so don't animate it until you are comfortable with your characters. This takes a while. The first shot you animate should probably be an easy one somewhere in the middle of the film. That way, you can get a feel for the characters before animating the critical shots. This also ensures that the end of your movie will look more fully resolved, because it will have been animated at the end of production, when everyone has become comfortable with the story, characters, and other elements.

Keeping Track of Things

After production begins laying out shots, you need to track each shot through the production process. This usually involves a bit of paperwork to ensure that everyone involved in production is kept up to date on the progress of the film.

A tracking sheet is a piece of paper or Web page on a computer that keeps track of each and every shot as it flows through the production. Different studios call these documents by different names—lead sheets, production tracking, and so on. Despite the differing terminology, they all keep track of basically the same information.

Tracking sheets are usually set up as tables. Each horizontal row contains the information for one shot. The vertical columns contain information for each step of the process. Typical columns might include modeling, texturing, rigging, layout, animation, and rendering. There may also be spaces for information such as the name of the animator, the number of revisions, and so on.

As each step is finished for each shot, the appropriate boxes are marked so that the director and producers can instantly see the progress of the film.

Rendering and Output

Once your animation is complete, you need to render it and output it to film or video. Film always looks great, particularly on the big screen. Unfortunately, you can't just hand people a 35mm print and tell them to go watch your film. Video is certainly a more practical medium, though it lacks the quality of film. You can also distribute your animation digitally on CD-ROM, on DVD, or over the Internet.

Output to Video

Video is the most common output for computer animation. Video output cards are very reasonably priced, making it by far the cheapest way to get your film into a format that people can see. You can simply print your video to a standard home video recorder, but this does not by any means give you the best-quality picture. Digital decks that use the DV tape format along with an IEEE1394 interface produce excellent-quality images.

Most post houses can also output your digital frames directly to higher-end formats like DigiBeta, D1, and HDTV. You can simply back up your frames to an archival medium such as CD-ROM or DLT tape and have the post house do the conversion and output for you.

Output to Film

Film is a great medium for output. Videotape formats seem to change with the seasons, but 35mm film has been constant for almost a century. Many major studios even go so far as to record their digitally created cartoons to film for archive, even though it is not needed for broadcast.

If you want to output to film, you open up a whole new can of worms. Film requires images of a much higher resolution than video. The typical film recorder requires an image that's at least 2048 lines wide, as opposed to video's 640 lines, taking up 10 times the storage space of video. This can blow your storage requirements through the roof. Film recorders can also be expensive to rent. Some companies, however, have set up service bureaus that can output film from your data on a per-frame basis.

To get your images to film, the typical process is to back up all the frames on an archival medium that the service bureau can read. DLT tape is the most popular format, because you can get more than 40GB on a tape. After the tape is in the proper format, you basically hand it to the bureau, and they give you back a negative of your film—and, of course, a bill.

Another way of getting film output is to print your animation to videotape, such as DigiBeta, and go to a service that prints video to film. This looks decent, but not nearly as good as a direct-to-film transfer. Some people are now using HDTV as the intermediate format. I've heard that this can work very well, particularly because HDTV can support 24fps.

Adding Sound Effects

Now that your film has been animated and rendered, you still need to do some postproduction to add sound effects and sync up the dialogue.

Creating good sound effects is an art in itself, and if you have the budget, a good sound engineer is worth the money. If you don't have that sort of budget, you can find plenty of sound effects CDs on the market with a wide variety of sounds, from realistic to cartoony.

There are also many times when you need sound effects that aren't in any collections. If this is the case, you need to create them from scratch. This involves setting up a microphone and recording the sounds you need. If you want the sound of breaking glass, for example, get a hammer and smash some pop bottles. (Wear safety glasses, of course!) You can be very creative in the types of objects you use to create your sound effects. Toys like slide whistles, kazoos, and jaw harps make great sounds. Also, atypical effects can make a scene much funnier. If a character runs into a wall, the sound of a bowling strike may be funnier than a simple thud.

One sound effect that is often overlooked is the ambient sound of the room. If you're in the city, the room may have faint echoes of traffic in the distance. Country dwellers may have birds or crickets as their background. This type of effect is barely audible but adds a subtle sense of space to the film.

How do you add sound effects? Well, a good recording studio with an engineer is the best way to do this. You are paying not only for the use of the studio's equipment, but for the engineer's time and expert ear. If you can't afford this, most video editing packages allow you to add a track of sound effects over the dialogue and sync it to video. More sophisticated multitrack sound editing software packages are geared specifically for the task of mixing sound for film. These packages allow you to mix dozens of digital tracks in real time as well as to add effects. The sound can then be mixed to a simple stereo or mono track and synced to your film in Premiere, or at a postproduction facility.

Distribution

After your film is complete, how do you get people to look at it? Well, if the film was a work-for-hire project for a studio or commercial client, that matter is pretty much out of your hands. The owner of the film handles the distribution.

If you have a student or personal film, distribution is very important. In the past, many people have sent films to film festivals. There are a number of major festivals, including Annecy in France, the LA Animation Celebration, and Hiroshima in Japan, as well as many, many more. Siggraph is a great festival for 3D animation.

One currently popular method of distribution is the Internet. Simply put up a Web site with a link to your film. Pass on the link to some of your friends. If they like it, they'll pass it on to their friends, and so on. Some films have really taken off through this word-of-mouth method. For more exposure, you might also consider a number of film sites on the Internet that take a cut of future proceeds in exchange for hosting your film.

Conclusion

Every animator needs to have directing and storytelling skills. As the "actors" in the story, the animators are the ones who are actually telling the story. An understanding of the way stories work will help your animation skills immensely. Write some stories on your own, using the techniques outlined in this chapter. Practicing the art of creating stories will make you a better storyteller.

The process of turning your stories into a film is always a big challenge, but you'll get an immense feeling of accomplishment once it's finished. The rewards can be great as well, since you'll have a product that you can use to sell your skills and further your career. Even if you create your film only for yourself, it will pay you back many times over in terms of knowledge and experience.

Index